KT-471-877

College of Ripon & York St. John
3 8025 00392029 8

Design Process

rogress Practice

Designmuseum

PUBLISHING CREDITS

Edited by James Peto, Design Museum
Design by Pentagram

Printed in Spain
Turner Libros S.A.
Zurbano, 10 - 2º
28010 Madrid

Published by
Design Museum
Shad Thames
London SE1 2YD
Tel. 0171 403 69 33
Fax 0171 378 65 40

ISBN 1 872005 40 3
D. L.: M-38062-1999

CONTRIBUTORS

Richard Seymour is a founding partner of the design consultancy, Seymour Powell, and is one of Europe's leading product designers.

James Dyson is the inventor of the Dual Cyclone™ vacuum cleaner and Chairman of Dyson Appliances.

Lesley Butterworth is Head of Education at the Design Museum.

Winfried Scheuer is an Industrial Designer, freelance writer and Professor of Industrial Design at the Kunstakademie, Stuttgart.

Roger Coleman is the Director of the Helen Hamlyn Research Centre at the Royal College of Art, London.

Eric Kentley is Assistant Director (Curatorial and Education Programme) of the Design Museum.

Perry King is a founding partner of King-Miranda Associati, Milan, and was until recently Visiting Professor at the School of Architecture and Design at the Royal College of Art, London.

Bill Moggridge is a founding partner and **Tim Brown** the European Director of the international design company IDEO.

Peter Quartermaine is a Research Associate at the National Maritime Museum, Greenwich, and Senior Lecturer in Postcolonial Studies at the University of Exeter.

Pauline Nee is Borough Architect and Building Surveyor, Southwark Building Design Service, London Borough of Southwark.

Introdu

ction

When the Design Museum first opened its doors to the public in 1989, it did so in both geographical and intellectual isolation. Standing on an undiscovered quayside in south London, it was the very first museum to champion mass production and industrial design at a time when the rest of the museum world had little interest. As the Museum's founder, Sir Terence Conran, stated: 'It always struck me as extraordinary that we had so many fantastic museums and galleries devoted to fine and decorative arts, and yet we took industrial design – which has a much more direct bearing on our lives – for granted'.

Ten years on, both the landscape and mindscape have altered fundamentally. The desolate area has transformed into one of London's most desirable areas. Design itself has become intellectually and museologically fashionable. New museums of design have sprung up around the world and many long-established art and decorative art museums have woken up to design as a subject of great popular interest.

However, the social environment has also changed fundamentally over the course of the decade. Inspiring an aesthetic appreciation of design is only one of the Museum's aims. As we move into the 21st century, we look to design to be not only aesthetically uplifting, but also environmentally and socially responsible. This means that the Museum must go beyond the examination of form and into the realms of inspiration, creativity and development – that is, examining what designers actually **do** and why.

For the Museum's tenth anniversary we have therefore chosen to mount an exhibition examining the design process in a wide range of disciplines. Curated by Eric Kentley, James Peto and Lesley Butterworth of the Design Museum, it raises fundamental questions about the nature of design. The following essays reflect the major themes of the exhibition.

Paul Thompson
Director

Richard Seymour

word you
know the
of until y
and defin

Design, a think you meaning ou try e it.

Design (di' zain) n,vb. a word you think you know the meaning of until you try to define it.

Like 'love', 'quality' and 'New Labour', design is one of those things that you are absolutely, positively sure you can define in a succinct little soundbite, but then find that the reality eludes you.

Try it....
go on,
I dare you.

The actual dictionary definition is as tortuous as it is dopey, and it runs to virtually three column inches, so don't feel bad if you come up with zip yourself. Better men than I have tried to nail this one down, but the lack of a specific, clear definition is one of the reasons why there is so much misunderstanding between clients and designers, between designers and engineers, and between your mum and her VCR.

It's actually much easier to say what design is not. It's not the rearranging of elements to come up with something that is worse than what was there before, although you'd hardly know that if you look around you. In my opinion there should be a new word that describes this form of bogus inanity (perhaps Douglas Adams could help out from The Meaning of Liff) that permanently brands the perpetrator.

Croydoning, perhaps...or maybe Towcestering, as in: "you are a complete **Towcester**".

Another thing it isn't is taking a straightforward, everyday object, painting it blue and calling it a 'designer' something. I believe the first appearance of this dreadful misappropriation in the public domain was when Vanderbilt 'designer' jeans appeared nearly twenty years ago. In creating this sub-definition, Gloria's advertising agency single-handedly diverted the definition to mean 'trivially reworked so that we can charge a bleeding fortune'.

Words such as 'clothes' and 'Emperor's new' spring to mind. Design should definitely not refer to the act of hoodwinking people into paying more than an object is actually worth...but here we get into dangerous territory. Isn't that what fashion is all about? Well, here we get to struggle with the first basic building blocks of what good design is about. There are physical and emotional rewards to the user in good design. What about that little light in a BMW limo that doesn't just 'go out' when you close the door, but which slowly dims in a stately and, frankly, luxurious manner?

Hmmmm.

Do you know anyone who doesn't like that? But what is its actual purpose? If you try to define this little confection in a logical way ('oh yeah, it's there to let your eyes adjust more easily to the change in light levels...') you won't get very far before someone pushes the bullshit button. But define it on a level of emotional satisfaction, like the reassuring clunk of the door closing or the languid, slow-mo ballet of a Nakamichi hi-fi cassette-door opening, and the picture becomes clearer. These are elements of what we at Seymour Powell call 'emotional ergonomics' and they are entirely legitimate aspects of good design. Let's look at some practical examples. Is an Alessi bottle opener (you know, the one that looks like a little devil) good design or bad design? Well, it works just as well as any other bottle-opener I've ever used, but it also makes me smile every time I open a bottle. It gives me a little wink when I'm at my most frazzled in the evening.

Yup. It passes the test.

It's effective and it engages my emotions. But what if it had still got that little bit of humour but it actually worked worse than its less amusing brethren? You'd feel that you had been taken for a ride, and you'd be right.

Think of the last thing that you bought just for the reason that you loved it. Was it that little black dress? Or that Audi TT (you wish)? Or that delightful little metal cell-phone? How does it make you feel when you use it?

Good. You pass the test, too.

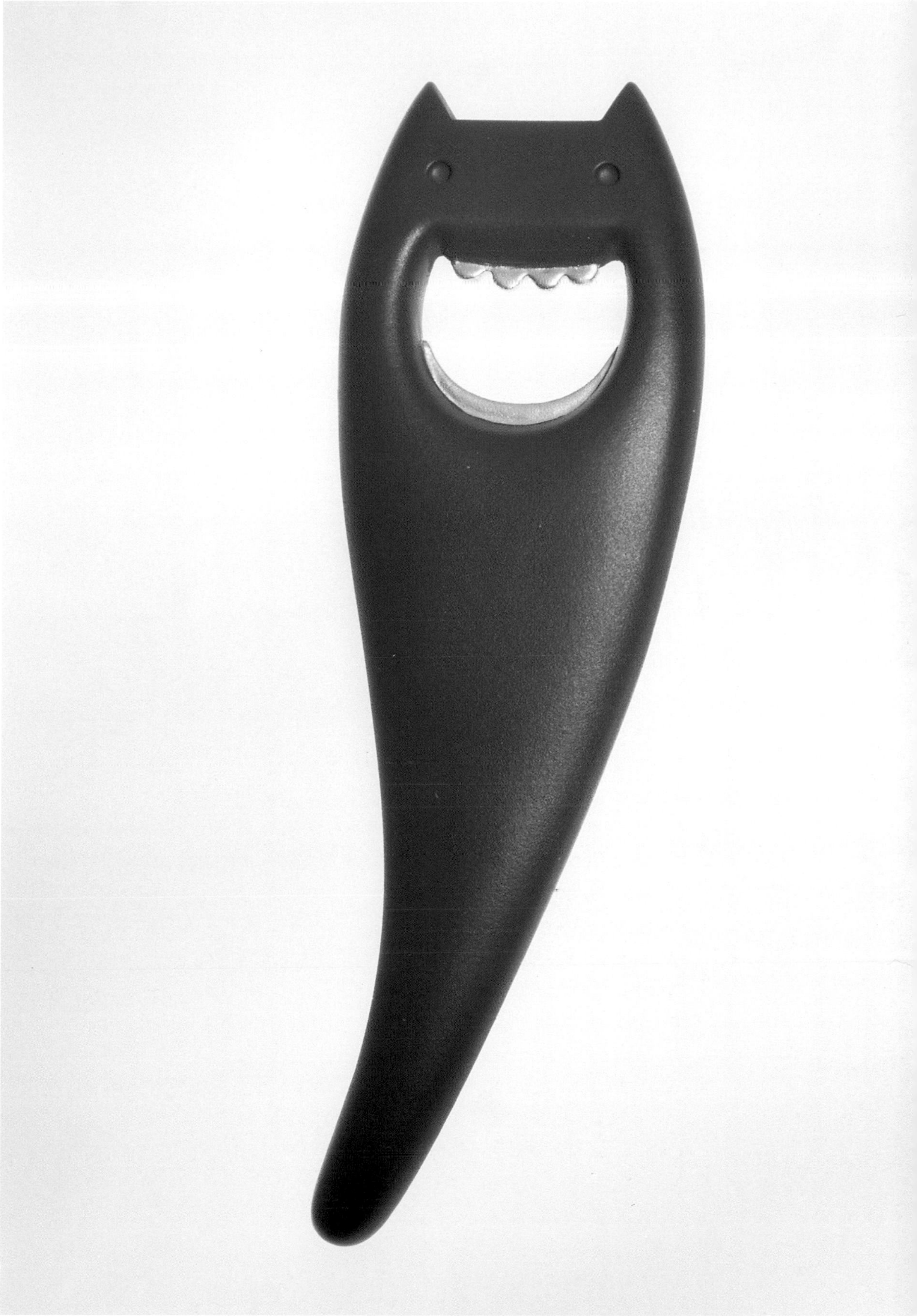

Alessi Bottle Opener – Try Hating It...

We need, as organisms, emotional as well as practical rewards in our lives, and it's the designer's job to deliver them. Why shouldn't things be a joy to own and use? Why shouldn't they bring emotional satisfaction? Anyone who's ever picked up a Fender Stratocaster (especially an old one) knows this feeling very well. The damn thing just drips with endorphins. You are probably as bad a guitarist as I am, but it doesn't matter: the magic just oozes out of the lacquer.

Just how this metaphysical component gets into a design is still a mystery to me. I know how it works, but I don't have any secret formula for producing it. Think carefully about the 'appeal' of an object the next time you're out shopping. Try to observe yourself in a clinical manner as you scan the shelves for the goodies. And when you find something that really gets your pulse racing, stop and try to understand what's happening to you.
Did you really go:

'wow...that's a really great looking wristwatch and I love it because it's all heavy-looking and obviously expensive'?

No, you didn't.

Your brain did a very interesting thing. It made an almost instantaneous analysis, at a subconscious level, and then pumped yum-juice into your limbic system until it lit up like a Christmas Tree.
You didn't actually think anything initially, you just felt it and it came out as a sort of 'I like it, I want it ...now what is it?' process, which your conscious mind then qualified.

No wonder we're such suckers

This burst of 'telemetry' that comes off any object when you first encounter it has a massive role to play in your comprehension of the rest of it, and it's totally tyrannical. Look at this object. →

What is it?

No ... it's a motorcycle.

But because your brains pan up the hard-drive in the belief that it was a bicycle, you are now slave to the preconception.

Intellectually, you can escape its gravitational force, but emotionally you find it very difficult. For example, what clothes would you wear to ride this motorcycle? Big black boots and a full-face helmet? I don't think so. Perhaps a little violet Spandex may put in an appearance here. And would you ever consider parking a motorcycle

in your house overnight to stop it being nicked? Not very likely. But what about a bicycle? You see? The appearance of the object has a huge effect on your comprehension and point of view. That's why I've always had trouble with the glib Modernist catch-phrase: "form follows function".

It doesn't, very often.

As my partner, Dick, once observed: Form IS function, or a very important part of it, anyway. It tells you how to use the thing, which way to hold it, where to start reading it, which end to drink from etc., etc.

Form informs.

And how it works with all the other more pragmatic and tangible components of the physical make-up of things is what keeps us all up late at night, trying to apportion the necessary elements in an acceptable manner. If you're a product designer, like me, you have to balance these factors carefully all the time.

Because a thing that looks nice but doesn't function practically is a sculpture.

And a thing that works but doesn't reward emotionally is a machine.

But a product designer, like any other designer, also has to think about how their idea will be made (be the thing a book or a baby buggy or a website). And if it costs a zillion pounds to make our bottle-opener out of pure unobtainium, then we fail the test again. Efficiency and, yes, simplicity is also part of our definition. Should we make an object more difficult to make just for the hell of it? No. Should we make an object more expensive to make because, in doing so, we make it much easier to use?

Well ... yes, I guess.

If I'm wrong, then you wouldn't be using that computer-driven, pocket camera that gives you a Patrick Litchfield-quality result from a single press of the shutter. Or that 'cordless' kettle you've got perched on your worksur-face, for that matter. There are more bits in cordless kettle than in a simple, 'plug in' one. But those extra bits make the object easier (and safer) to use.

So, is an engineer a designer? Yes. Engineering is part of the act of design (although there are probably some middle-aged, agitated individuals out there who would happily feed me through their bandsaw for saying it). And invention is also part of the act of design. Part of the problem with the definition here is that it isn't inclusive, and that's partly a historical issue.
Is James Dyson an inventor, a manufacturer or a designer?

He's an inventive designer, who also makes things.

Is Trevor Bayliss an inventor or designer?

He's an inventor.

There are still many engineers who turn up their noses at certain 'designers' because they see them as effete pansies who just make things 'look nice'. And there are probably an equal number of 'designers', who are more occupied, perhaps, with the way in which the object communicates through its appearance, and its emotional relevance to the user, who think that pure engineers are a bunch of...gits!

Listen up, both parties. That's like saying that the yoke of an egg is more important than the white, or that a Ferrari's drive-train is more important than its trouser-filling curves.

It takes all of these things, working in harmony, to create really good design. Sometimes, rarely, all of the relevant skills exist within a single individual. The God of motorcycle design, Massimo Tamburini, is one of these rare individuals. Engineer, inventor and, what the hell, style diva in one compact organism. He is personally responsible for some of the most drop-dead gorgeous, fastest, best-handling Italian machines on the planet.

What is he? He's a designer.

Someone who balances efficiency, innovation, manufacturability, Young's modulus and visceral, emotional appeal all at the same time.

We lesser mortals have to put up with a smaller deck, but we've still got to be sensitive to all of those issues or the thing goes belly-up. The real trick is in

Ducati 916
God's Gift to Motorcyclists
from the Man Himself.

SP toilet for Channel 4 – "Nobody's going to pay more for a toilet that cleans itself..."

knowing the proportional balance of these individual factors. It has often been said that design is about compromise. That you can't have something that doesn't short-change at least one of these critical factors.

But I'm an optimist. I don't think in terms of compromise, but in terms of equilibrium. In a recent television series, my partner, Dick Powell and I had to face some pretty hairy design problems: but they weren't half as hairy of some of the dogma we had to face.

When confronted with the problem of designing a better toilet, we had to go right back to first principles. In doing so, we found a number of what we call 'standing waves' in the evolution of the toilet from its first beginnings to the devices we know and love today. Because of some early decisions made back there in the mists of time, toilets were made, effectively, to sit on, not to pee into from a great height when you are full of lager. Also, they were not configured to take a seated male in an, how can I say this, optimal fashion. When we created a new toilet that made it easier to sit on, pee into, flush and keep clean, the reaction from the client was bewildering: 'Nobody's going to pay more for a toilet that cleans itself' were the words of the Marketing Director (going from memory). The fact that, at that stage, he had no idea what the cost implications of these modifications were, made his remarks all the more extraordinary.

But, having thought about this issue at length since, I can now see his point of view. He didn't actually want a better toilet. He wanted a conventional toilet that performed in an entirely conventional manner at a particular price-point in the marketplace. Because he was sure he could sell that.

Not for nothing do we fear change.
Change means risk.

So, by definition, design must also mean risk, because whatever definition of design we get to in all this, it's going to have to incorporate the concept of change. To me, in this particular context, change meant better in virtually every axis of our developing picture of design. Perhaps we were being naïve in our balance of factors? Nope.

Have you any idea how much of your life is spent on a toilet? Or how much of your life is spent cleaning it? Toilets are unusual artefacts. They're permanent (unless you've got a particularly violent enteric disorder). Normally, the only reason you have to change them is that you don't like the colour or the style of the one you already have. A small price hike, coupled with a body of development work on the manufacturing side is, in my book, a small price to pay for permanent comfort and cleanliness.

What I think was wrong in the equation was that the client hadn't fixed his eyes on what would provide him with a very robust design philosophy into the future: the need to make things better for people.

The Japanese motorcycle manufacturers understood this philosophy in the early 1970s, which is how they managed to virtually wipe the rest of the world's manufacturers off the map for a time. Up until the Japanese invasion, British manufacturers were making things that they wanted to make. But Honda and Kawasaki, soon to be followed by Yamaha and Suzuki, realised that they needed to make things that people wanted to buy.

It would be ridiculous to suggest that British manufacturers weren't in a position to fit electric starters, indicators and leak-proof, oil-tight engines to their machines if they'd had a mind to. But they didn't, and the Fire from the East swept across them. They didn't because they didn't think it was that important.

But it was.

If they'd understood the latent desire among their market for these things, they'd have probably got there first.

But they didn't.

If you stand inside any industry, you'll find that your view out into the rest of the world is somewhat limited. For some reason, much corporate culture acts as a sort of psychotropic drug, which detaches the brain from the heart. If anyone from BSA had been in the same frame of mind on a Monday morning as they were on the previous Saturday evening as they'd tried to kick-start their wretched, leaky twin into a semblance of life, then they would have seen this. If the same person had looked away from their motorcycle and at the car parked next to them, they'd have seen this also. The same goes for the sanitary-ware client, as he scrubbed away diligently at his toilet at home.

The same goes for the fool who designed the system for programming your video machine, or who created the corned-beef can or (insert most hated product characteristic here).

It's crucially important to begin with the end-user when you design absolutely anything. If the VCR engineers had spent just a little time considering timer programming from a human point of view, then we wouldn't have had to put up with twenty years of bullshit. Whose idea was it that a bra should fasten at the back? What meathead decided to put anti-arthritis pills in a childproof container? Or to put the instructions for an emergency eye-wash bottle in 6 point type?

We laugh, don't we? But it isn't funny. Not even a little bit...only a complete Towcester would be so crass and unthinking.

Corned Beef –
The Terminator

The best design comes from thinking like a person, not a job description.

The best design comes from finding the things that bring us grief, that make our lives worse, not better, and fixing them.

Replacing drudgery with fun.

Replacing mind-numbing complexity with elegant simplicity, whenever you can.

Replacing ugliness with beauty.

Making things better. For people.

Perhaps we could put this in the dictionary instead.

James Dyson

A Res
to a

ponse

Problem

At Dyson we create and build products: that's how we make our living. We don't try to remould or rebrand existing products. We are not concerned with empty styling. We want to create innovative products with revolutionary technologies that work better for the people who use them. This takes hard work, not flashes of brilliance. Thinking creatively and working in unconventional ways means we can design and manufacture products with a difference.

I developed the technology for the Dyson Dual Cyclone™ vacuum cleaner in response to a problem. Vacuuming the home one Saturday morning I noticed that the bag cleaner I was using wasn't sucking properly. I assumed this was because the bag was full. I couldn't find a new bag in the house so I emptied the old one, taped it together again, put it back in the machine and switched it on. It still wouldn't pick up. Looking at the bag again more closely I saw that it was empty except for a layer of dust coating the inner surface.

That's when I understood how the vacuum cleaner worked.

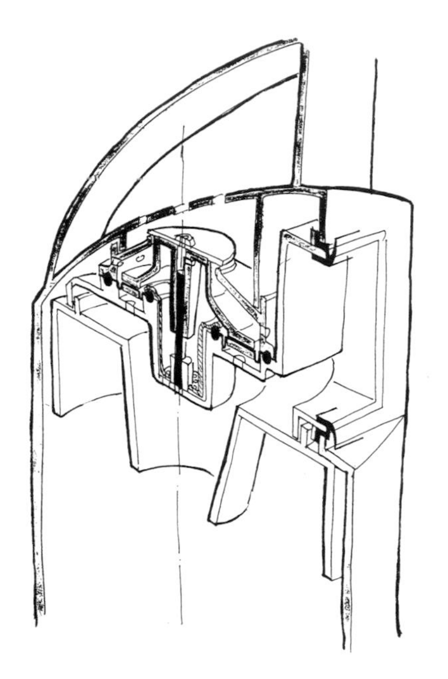

The bag wasn't simply a collection device; it was a big filter. The motor created the airflow through the machine (i.e. the suction), but the dust-laden air had to pass through the bag in order to filter out the dust. However the fine particles of dust quickly clogged the pores in the walls of the bag that the air was supposed to pass through, causing a loss of airflow, and therefore loss of suction and loss of pick up. This was when I began to think differently about the vacuum cleaner and this is what drove my search for a different filtration system. It was a long process.

I had seen cyclone filters in operation before. We had built one to extract excess paint from the spray chamber in the ball barrow factory, based on those that can be found on top of saw mills. I set about making this principle work in a vacuum cleaner. Having had the initial idea I then had to develop a satisfactory working prototype.

5,127
iterations later,
I produced
the Dual
Cyclone™

This works by using two cyclones to filter out the dust from the airflow. The first cyclone spins the larger particles of dust and dirt out of the air, the second, smaller, faster cyclone separates out the minuscule dust particles from the airflow.

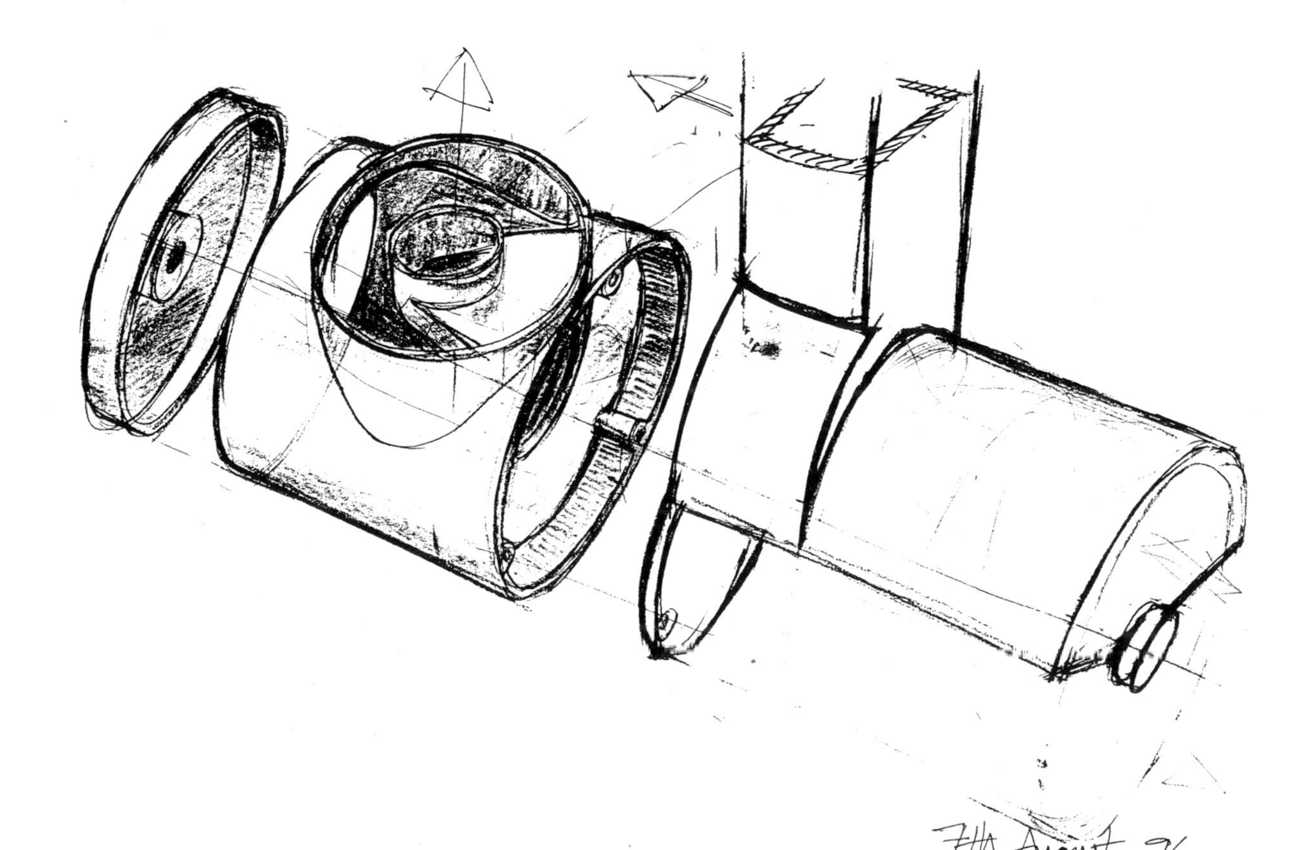

Prototype for the DC03

This iterative approach is how all design engineers work at Dyson. When designing a new product, engineers begin by describing a brief that is a response to their own ideas and often suggestions from users of previous products. When we began work on DC03 we knew that we wanted to develop a slim-line, lighter, quieter and more powerful upright vacuum cleaner that used Dual Cyclone™ technology.

Engineers start generating concepts by quickly producing a large number of sketches in response to the brief. This produces a wide range of ideas; for example the stair-hugging shape of DC02 originated at this stage. Then they are able to write a detailed design specification setting out all the key design features they want to include. Balancing ideas about function, safety, reliability, aesthetics and cost is a complex process.

During development engineers make hundreds of different prototypes in order to test out their ideas. This is where the 'Edisonian approach' is so important. Using a variety of prototypes such as cardboard, blue foam, breadboard and fuse deposition modelling in conjunction with sketches and CAD, engineers test their ideas against the original specification. They only ever make one change at a time. This is slow, but necessary. It is the only way of knowing if the change has made an improvement. We apply this process to the development of all our new products, for example the DC03.

After the launch of our first upright and cylinder vacuum cleaners we felt we wanted to produce another, very different upright. Historically, upright vacuum cleaners have been big, brutish and powerful. Lighter, smaller uprights were cheap, low tech, usually poor in performance and unappealing visually. There was no market for a top of the range, light, slim upright. Yet at Dyson we felt that a product like this would be very well received by, for example, older consumers who wanted a lighter machine or people who had limited storage space. We also knew we could persuade the European market, which favours smaller machines, to buy one that used new technology and worked well. We had no statistics to prove it, but our instincts told us that we could make it a commercial success.

Part of our confidence came from the close links engineers

The DC03 Clear

have with customer care. We get a great deal of feedback from our consumers in this way and we knew that people had suggested a lighter machine that went flat under furniture. So we designed DC03 to be very slim. The depth of the machine is dictated by the diameter of the motor driving the brush-bar and the cyclone. We worked hard with our suppliers to push the limits of the design of the motor. The result was a lightweight, low-diameter, high-efficiency motor that meant we could reduce the depth of the cleaner and the size of the mouldings around the motor itself.

The DC03 has the highest filtration of any vacuum cleaner. We were determined to achieve a lifetime post-filter and year-long pre-filter. This meant the filters were much bigger than those we had used before, yet we were trying to design a less bulky machine. Our solution was to design it with twin cylinders and an asymmetric form. The clear plastic housing minimised the visual impact of the large filters. The clear bin also contributes to the overall visual lightness of the machine.

Perhaps the most noticeable innovations on the DC03 are the clutch mechanism and the brush-bar that can be switched on or off. We knew from working closely with customer care that a common problem with all upright vacuum cleaners is the broken belt. This usually occurs as a result of something jamming the brush-bar or getting wrapped round it. The clutch component on DC03 acts as an override in these instances and the noise of the ratchet, which turns instead of the belt to prevent it breaking, lets you know that something is wrong. The clutch component has the added advantage of allowing consumers to switch the brush-bar off when vacuuming delicate floor coverings.

We developed a special bleed valve on DC03 in order to maintain the airflow and efficiency of the cyclone. This pressure-balanced valve sustains the cyclone efficiency by allowing the right amount of air in at all times. This makes the machine much more efficient. We could reduce the amount of power the motor had to input, but managed to get more work out of it: the airflow was much more efficient meaning that the suction and pick-up were much more powerful.

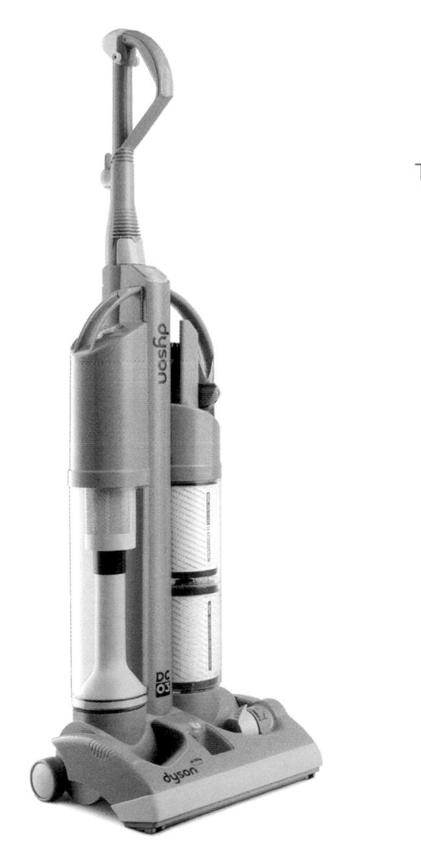

The DC03

The DC04

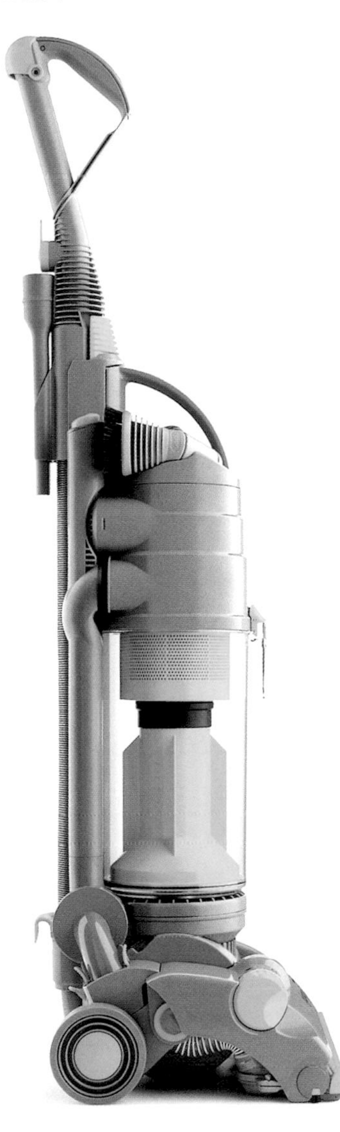

The handle on DC03 is designed to make carrying the machine easier and has the advantage of allowing this lightweight cleaner to hang flat from a hook in the wall or door. The capped end is a detail developed in response to comments from users of DC01. By taking the handle on DC03 away from the airway and

giving it an ergonomic grip we made the machine more pleasing to use.

We had looked carefully at how vacuum cleaners are used and noted how often people had to bend down to change floor tools that were stored at the base of the machine. On DC03 we wanted to have the tools stored close to hand and worked hard to design a solution. They now fit conveniently on the top of the filter cover.

Finally, we also made the bin easier to empty. DC03 has one button that releases the bin and cyclone assembly, which can then be taken out to the dustbin for emptying as a self-contained unit.

Our design engineers are driven by their own ideas, customer feedback and developments in supplies and materials. Since the launch of DC01, innovations in materials such as ABS meant that colourings could be introduced without compromising the strength of the plastic. We had already used translucent colour plastics on the DC02 Clear model and we wanted to revisit this idea with the DC03. In fact the DC02 Clear caught the eye of the design team at Apple. At their request we sent them a DC02 Clear, providing the inspiration for the iMac computer. We made DC03 Clear completely translucent in order to lay bare the function of the machine. Users of the machine tell us they enjoy being able to see every component working, right down to the motor and the clutch.

The whole development process, on which Dyson engineers spent a great deal of time and thought, is hugely complex. Step by step, and with testing at every stage, engineers developed the finished product.

To create a product with a difference it is vital to create a working culture where people are not afraid to take the risks inherent in trying something really new. It's always easy to think why a new idea might fail. Bankers and accountants armed with conclusive figures point to the risks, marketing people will show why a product will not sell by conducting focus groups. However, I like to do the opposite of what a focus group says;

people want to be surprised not bored.

People told us that a vacuum cleaner with a clear bin would never catch on. They said people would never want to see the dirt. Now, users of Dyson vacuum cleaners tell us they like to be able see how much dirt they have vacuumed up. Sometimes imagination is more important than knowledge.

Our engineers work alongside scientists in the Research and Development centre. These people also run teams, make financial decisions and are fully involved in every step of the design and manufacturing process.

The DC05

Why should companies be led by accountants, lawyers and salesman? Empowering engineers and designers means that team leaders provide inspiration, not just balance sheets. In this way design engineers know and understand what people might buy, understand the technology that is able to produce it, know how it could be made, what it would cost and what customers would be prepared to pay for it. When the engineers themselves take the responsibility for taking risks, then mistakes are not feared, only learnt from. Mistakes are an important part of the learning process of research and development (R & D), and only companies led by engineers will move on positively through them, rather than pulling up at the first sign of trouble.

In this way we are also able to build up a body of intellectual property. A good indicator of the health, inventiveness and solidity of a country's industry is the number of patents it files each year. In recent research on world patent activity the UK comes eleventh with 7.93 registrations per 100,000, trailing behind countries like Japan, Germany, Taiwan and Switzerland. These countries know the importance of continuous, active development, and of never letting up. They appreciate that small, step-by-step improvements add up, in the long term, to massive improvements that generate patents and ultimately the ownership of technology. Those of us involved in R & D know that it is not the brilliance of the quantum leap that should be admired, but dogged persistence.

Nationally, civil R & D expenditure as a proportion of Gross Domestic Expenditure decreased each year between 1993 and 1996. In 1996 only 26% of that R & D was funded by the government.* Having a solid base of investment in R & D at Dyson means that we are learning about new technology, enabling us to approach the design and engineering of a product differently and laterally. The working environment also plays an important role in this. It is crucial that engineering and design are not viewed as separate. There are no barriers between the disciplines of designing, engineering, scientific research, model-making, testing and machining. Everyone in every department should understand every part of the process. Engineers have access to all our research into new technologies. The offices are open plan to encourage communication and make everyone feel part of the same team.

This aesthetic and creative environment means that employees are able to concentrate their minds on engineering, testing and quality control. In this way Dyson design engineers are allowed to be free thinkers who take the company forward and have truly creative, revolutionary ideas.

There is a lot of talk about creativity in design. Yet young people leaving education today talk of wanting to go into the 'creative' industries of media

The DC02 Clear

and advertising. In fact 55% of all graduates want to choose media as a career while the number of applicants for engineering degrees is down 30% year on year. Design engineers at Dyson are engaged in the core creative task of making products that are used in people's homes every day. We need to show young people that the media and advertising industries are built on the backs of the industries creating and making real things. If we really want Britain to become a creative force again then we have to make people understand that, unlike advertising creatives, engineers create real things. Industry should do better to make clear that manufacturing and bringing products to the marketplace is a hugely exciting activity: it is fun, creative and involves high risk gambling based on judgement and intuition. In industry the stage is always changing and the players must do the same. You can never rest but must always be thinking of new ways to challenge established beliefs, prejudices and ways of working. When you compare this with how staid and mundane some other professions are, it should be easy to encourage young people to want to become designers and engineers. In turn, schools, colleges and universities must work to break down the preconceptions and barriers. Why is it that the British think the intelligentsia should not make things with their hands? Innovation at Dyson happens in the workshop, not the office.

All of this will require a dramatic change in our national attitudes. We have to inspire a passion for making things and a curiosity about how they might be made to work better. We need to create incentives for research and development spending and put creativity back into industry. We need to inspire and empower scientists and engineers to develop new technology to solve problems. We need to ignite enthusiasm in manufacturers so that they develop products they love with a sensitivity to the market. We need confidence so that we can reassure ourselves that we will achieve our goals.

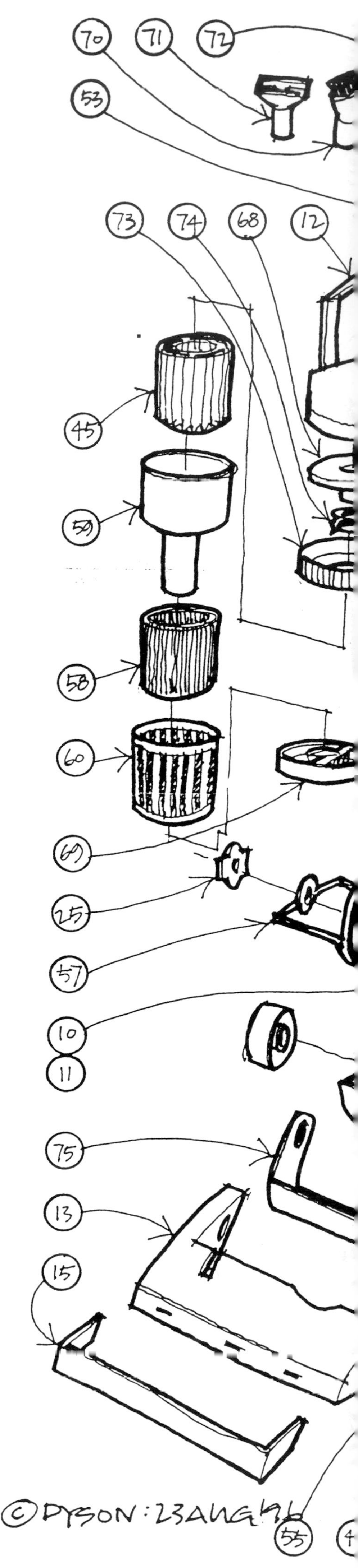

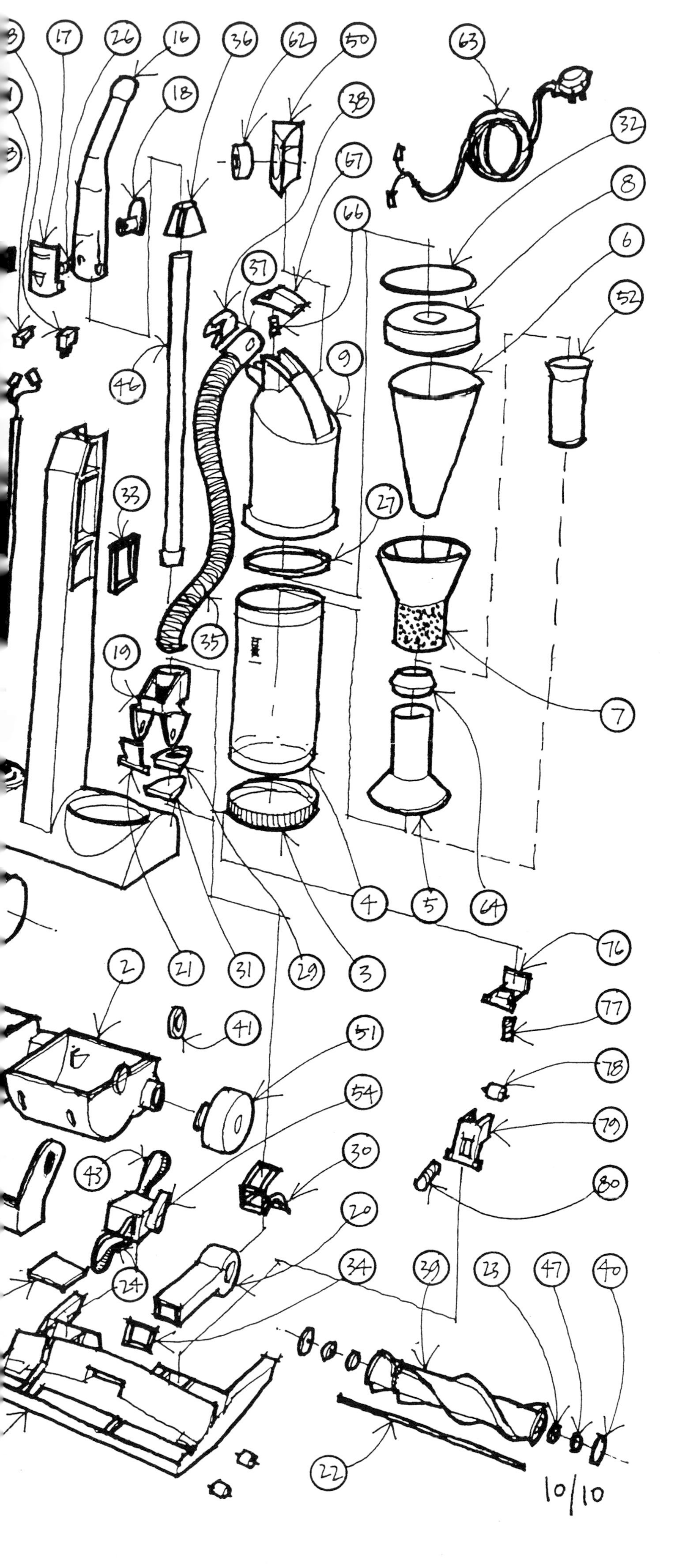

Creativity is a socially and economically cohesive force.

Design and engineering are creative activities that allow people to express their individuality and imagination. We need to engender a new sense of hope within the industry so that we can dare to be different once again.

*ONS statistics: Business Enterprise Research and Development 1997

Lesley Butterworth

within the

the Desig

Drawing
Context of
n Process

In 1886 Gustav Eiffel sketched, in pencil, an idea for 'Gallia, Metal Tower, 300 metres high'. This was the first sketch of what was to become the Eiffel Tower, completed in 1889. The sketch is lively and animated, showing the tower much as it appeared in the finished version, with a landscape lightly intimated between the arches. The use of weight of line in the sketch shows the patterns created by the metal framework.

If this was the first sketch of the Eiffel Tower, it was not to be the last.

Many more drawings followed, engineering drawings, elevations, diagrams for the erection of the frame and for the establishment of the foundations.

After its completion the Eiffel Tower fast became a subject for artists such as the Post-Impressionist Georges Seurat, and fellow artists Robert Delauney and Douanier Rousseau.

The purposes of this essay are threefold. First; to define the nature of drawing. Second; to look at how designers use drawing as part of the design process, and third; to consider the position and historical impact of the drawings of designers alongside those of fine artists and architects. By placing these drawings in an exhibition the Design Museum is implying a certain status that has hitherto been unrecognised. This will I hope pave the way for further interest in this area of the work of a designer.

What is drawing?

As children we start to draw before we learn to read and write. I emphasise the word 'start'. Drawing is not taught as formally or as rigorously as writing, yet drawing is the earliest language, the oldest art form and the most accessible way of communicating. Drawing is the most immediate way of conveying an idea in pictorial terms. It requires a mark-making instrument, and a plain surface. Drawing can be both copying and creating. It can be as simple a message as where to put the shelves on a wall, a sketch for a potential product or painting, or a finished piece of work in its own right. It can be the process by which designers get the idea out of their heads and on to the drawing board. It makes ideas visible using a visual language, and can be a simple tool to learn and apply. It provides something to discuss, and kicks off the debate.

Drawing can be seen as the most fundamental activity of the designer, a selection of lines, made after great consideration, or very spontaneously. It can produce form, structure, solutions, inventions, and provide a starting point to a whole range of developments. Yet artists and designers do not just draw what they see, they draw to convention, or to a system. There are several drawing systems that designers might use. Differing drawing methods have developed through history, bound up with the development of drawing instruments and ways of seeing.

A projection system depends upon the idea of straight projection lines running from points on an object to corresponding points

on a flat surface. Early examples of this can be found in paintings on Greek vases during the fifth century BC.

Projection systems include orthographical, isometric and oblique projection.

Perspective is based on the principle that parallel lines converge on a single point, the central vanishing point, and the spectator should use one fixed point for his or her observation. First examples of perspective have been attributed to the mathematician Ptolemy in the second century AD, but it was the artist Paolo Uccello, and the architect Filippo Brunelleschi, who laid down the principles for perspective as a natural outcome of the developments in thirteenth-century Italy during the Renaissance.

Several drawing systems can be used simultaneously in one drawing. This can create an infinite variety of illusions, distortions and abstractions, can cross cultural and historic boundaries, and give the artist or designer a greater degree of manipulation, at the risk of the drawing looking 'wrong'. This use of drawing is mirrored by the breaking away from

The Eiffel Tower, 1889 (panel)
Georges Seurat
Fine Art Museums of San Francisco

representative art in the late nineteenth century, and the response by artists and designers to Cubism, Modernism and Abstract Expressionism in the early twentieth century. Artists such as Georges Braque, Paul Cézanne and Pablo Picasso used a variety of drawing systems, manipulating surface reality to create a personal visual expression.

It is clear that how we look and how we draw is governed by our position in history and culture, and it is interesting to see how the design profession has contributed to, and in many places led the way in directing, this process of change and development.

The Renaissance saw a move away from the medieval concept of God towards a more absorbing interest in and an examination of the skills and ambitions of humanity. Medieval draughtsmen worked from pattern books, and the naturalistic style, combined with the rapid development of perspective, is a major legacy of the Renaissance and perhaps one of the key moments in the practice and appreciation of drawing, comparable to the impact of the Industrial Revolution in the nineteenth century, and Modernism in the twentieth century.

The work of Leonardo Da Vinci, whose interests ranged from engineering to botany to painting and anatomy, exemplifies the searching outlook of the Renaissance and new ways of drawing. Figures and objects acquired a greater sense of

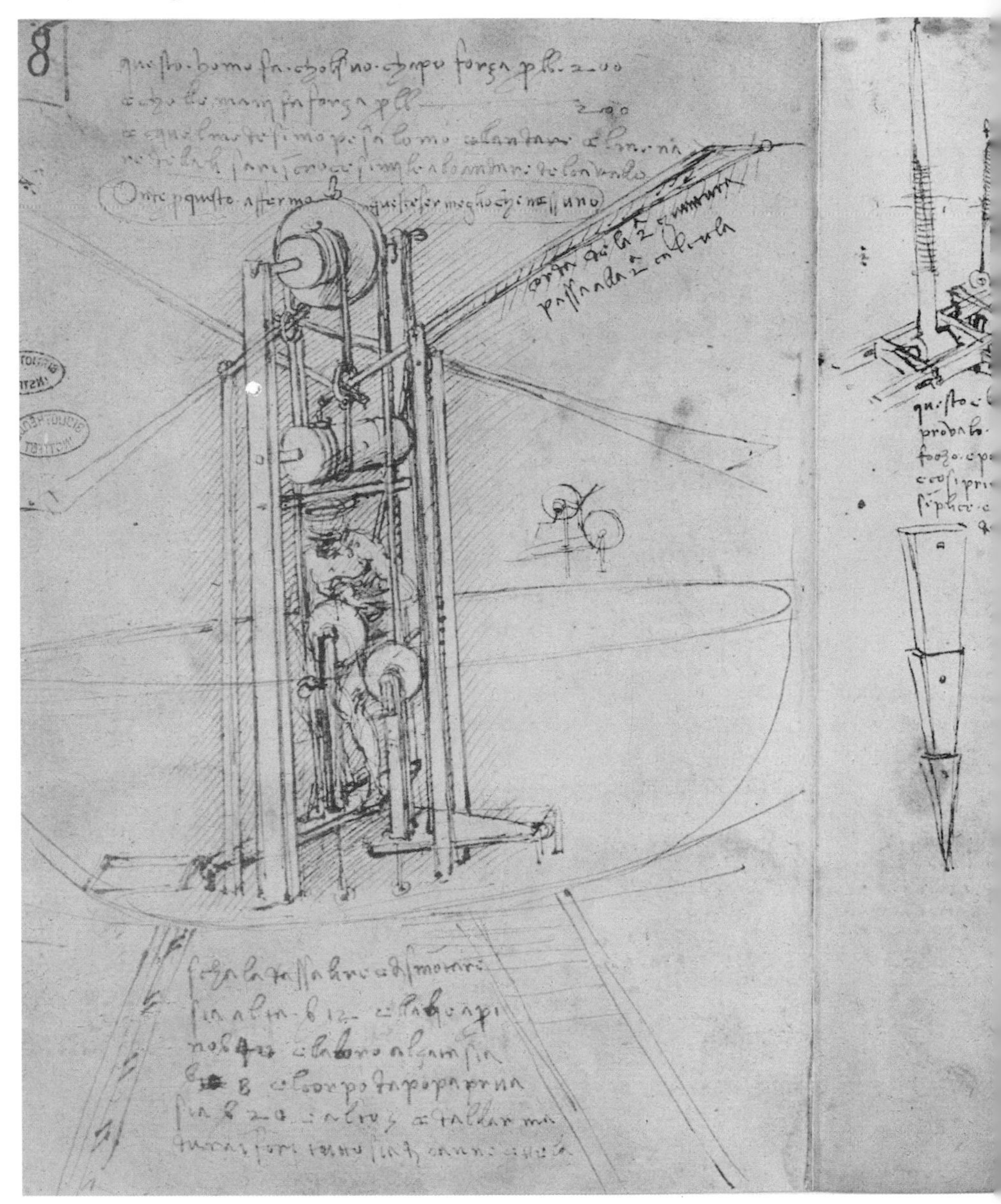

Diagram of Flying Machines, 1488
Leonardo da Vinci
Bibliothèque de L'Institut de France/
Lauros-Giraudon

plasticity and volume and were placed in settings where the dimensional space was defined with increasing clarity. Artists and designers began to transcribe what they perceived, rather than relying on handed down conventions. The use of drawing became synonymous with investigating nature, experimenting with

geometry,

right
Old London, 1493
woodcut, German School
from the *Nuremberg Chronicle*
by Hartman Schedel
Guildhall Library, Corporation of London

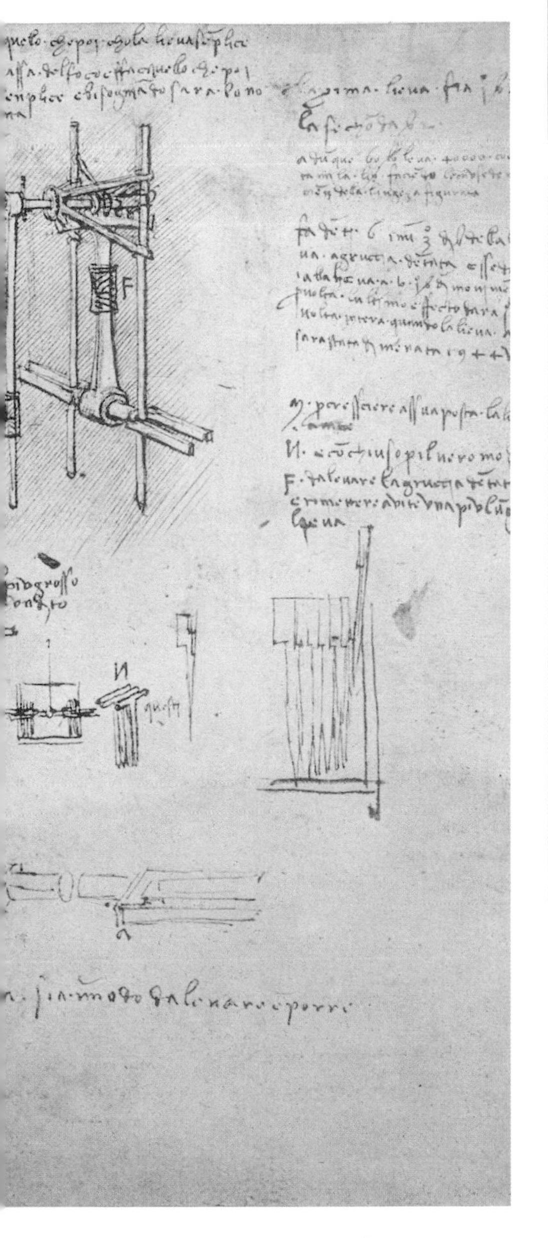

and the free expression of the imagination, and was to dominate both Western art and design and Western education until the nineteenth century.

If artists and architects were instrumental in changing the nature of drawing in the thirteenth century, then map makers were to contribute to the general development of drawing systems in the sixteenth century. The designers allied to the cartographic houses of Nuremberg were working on maps of the world in globular projection, an advanced form of perspective.

above
J.B. Homann, Nuremberg
O'Shea Gallery, London

perspective,
proportion,
composition,
perceptual aids

From the late eighteenth century onwards, the work of mechanical and civil engineers dominated and informed the development of drawing. The Industrial Revolution introduced new forms of production and manufacture, which in turn dictated differing working methods. In 1773 Matthew Boulton and James Watt set up the world's first factory for the construction of stationary steam engines in Birmingham. James Watt was the main draughtsman and he is particularly responsible for the rapid development of the engineering drawing from this time forward.

The period of peace and prosperity after the Industrial Revolution led to an increase in consumer spending, encouraging mass production for mass consumption. Textile and graphic designers, product designers and artists contributed to developments in drawing as a response to the teachings of the Bauhaus and the Modern movement.

The history of drawing is bound up with the history of design and the social, economic, technological and cultural changes of the centuries.

How do designers draw and use drawing as part of the design process? How essential is drawing to the design profession, given that designers are working in disciplines including architecture, engineering, fashion, product design, graphics and interior design?

Nigel Coates
Concept Sketch for the Body Zone
of the Millennium Dome, London, 1998

The artist Richard Long creates works that describe his physical relationship with the drawing surface. Long has walked across a field of thick wet grass and described the marks that he left as a drawing. This is a visual statement in its own right. No one can create anything more from it, apart from the artist, whose work will continue to develop.

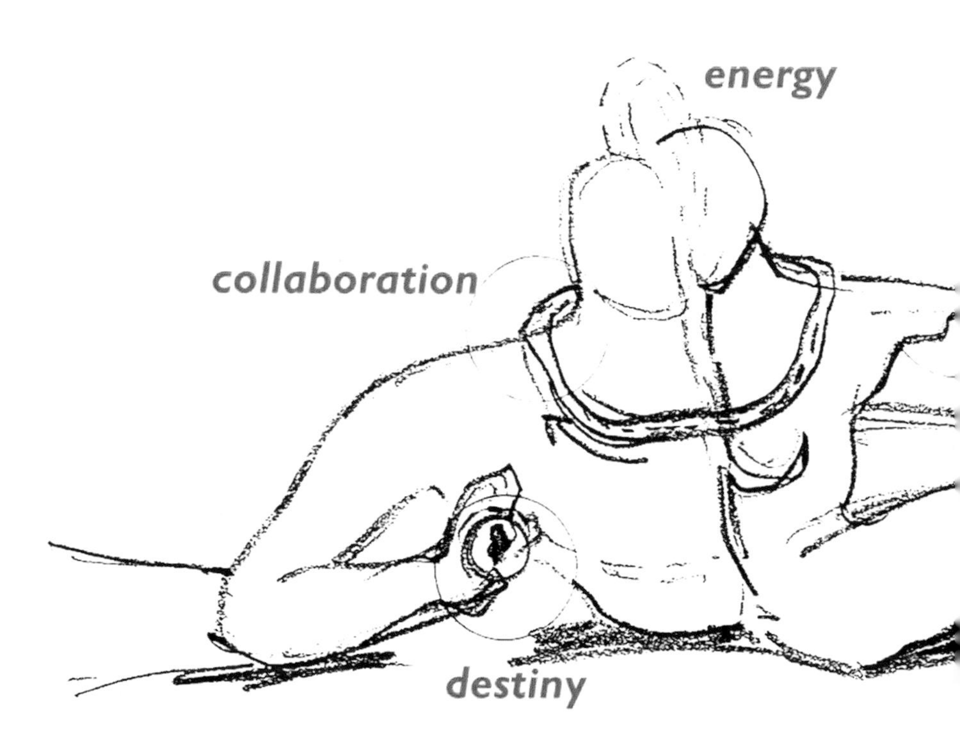

Drawing can both explain and express the barriers between subject areas.

An engineer will prepare a drawing for someone else to work from. The drawing will give specific technical information. The drawing will be depended upon for the correct instructions. This may seem far removed from the work of Richard Long, but in 1968 the artist Sol Le Witt gave a set of instructions for three drawings to be created on a gallery wall; this did not require the artist to be present. Draughtsmen were employed to execute the drawings, the finished art work.

Drawing, in a variety of forms, exists as an integral part of the design process. The design process itself varies from discipline to discipline, and it is impossible to illustrate here how drawing fits into each and every one. The design process is not as linear a progression as the next part of the essay intimates, but what follows is an attempt to show the position of drawing within the development, or redevelopment, of a design.

There are many different types of drawings that designers might engage in. The first drawing might be a sketch. Sketchbooks are a working tool for a designer, a place to collect, collate and analyse information, a repository for research. They help to form ideas and understanding, and to clarify problems and concerns. A sketchbook logs the development of ideas, some to be worked up, some to be discarded. A sketchbook can be seen as a visual diary, or a major research document.

From the initial sketch, one of many ideas from a sketchbook, done probably for the designer's attention alone, there may follow a concept drawing. The designer or design practice will receive a design brief from a client, or will have a predetermined project to work upon. They could be creating the Autumn collection for a fashion house. They could be an architectural practice responding to a competition, or a product design team working on domestic appliances. After consideration of the brief, a team or teams may be set up to work towards a solution. The concept drawing is the logical next stage in the drawing process. If a sketch is generalised research and inspiration, then the concept drawing is the first vision or solution to the brief on paper.

The concept drawing will be produced in whatever medium the designer favours: coloured pencils, felt pens, pen and ink and wash, and will provide a starting point for discussion with the design team. A concept drawing may not necessarily be to scale. It may include written notes, diagrams and measurements. It will not be the final description of the product, but in retrospect will provide a fascinating insight into what the product might have looked like. A designer or design team might produce a series of concept drawings as they work their way towards a solution. The concept drawings show the start of the evaluation process and may be accompanied by three-dimensional models.

Following on from the concept drawing comes the presentation drawing, a sophisticated image needed to sell the product back to the client. If the concept drawing is the first idea, then

Sketch for the Citroën 2CV

the presentation drawing has to say why

and be readable to a wider audience than the in-house design team. The presentation drawing will include careful colouring and rendering, and will be highly finished. A designer or design company may have a 'house style' for presentation drawings, and drawing skills themselves are valued at this stage; skills such as composition and use of colour, and the ability to work competently with an airbrush, or provide a computer visualisation. The presentation drawing may not show how every nut and bolt works (the client will probably neither want nor need this information), but will give an overall impression of the final look of the product.

If the presentation drawing 'sells' the idea to the clients, then that is its function completed. What it will not do is describe to engineers or production managers how the product works. This is the role of production drawings. A decision will be made to go ahead with a product, to concept and prototype stage, and into final production with the necessary tooling equipment as part of this process. The presentation drawing will have been successful in satisfying the client, but further drawings will be required to describe to model-makers and production managers how the product works and how it will be made. Engineering drawings and general arrangement drawings have a position here and, again, are quite distinctive from the drawings that have preceded them in the design process.

An engineering drawing may not be done by the originating designer, but by an engineer on the design team. It will not need to explain itself to anyone but a professional, but will have its own aesthetic qualities. Engineering drawings are executed in orthographic projection, by ink or pencil on film. The drawing may include pictorial views in perspective, and technical information.

A general arrangement drawing will provide a view of each of the component parts of the product, including overall dimensions, and how parts will interlock and interface. Produced in pen and ink on film, general arrangement drawings might give information about the material that each part will be made from, and details of tooling equipment needed for its manufacture. As with engineering drawings, general arrangement drawings will provide highly technical information for professional manufacturers, probably unreadable to an untrained eye. Yet again, they have their own aesthetic.

Nigel Coates
Schiphol Airport, Amsterdam, 1993

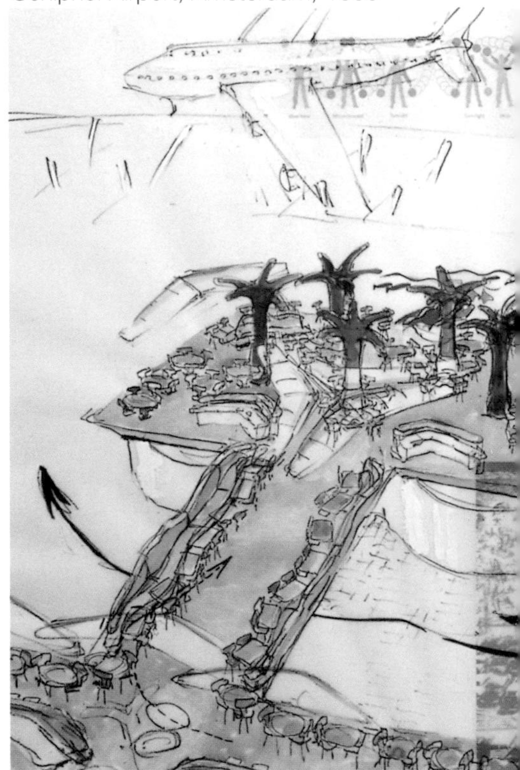

The product is now ready for final production. Concurrent with the design process of the product, a marketing department will have been at work overseeing the launch and advertising of the product. Some of the designer's drawings may be used in the advertising campaign. Very few products can move into the market place without instructions to the end user. At a simple level, a dress will require cleaning information. A more complex product, such as a car, a power drill or a camera, will be accompanied by information on the use and maintenance of

the product, and this invariably involves a series of drawings, probably linear and technical, that will explain how to load the film in the camera or replace the wheel on the car. In the global marketplace, the drawing is the ideal international language.

The description of the design of a product in this essay is intended to give a general impression, rather than a definitive overview of the design process. But even within such a broad description, it is possible to see how drawing, by pencil or pen, computer or airbrush, has both a critical position within the design process and a significant position in the history of the way objects are presented and how people see.

Museums and galleries frequently display the drawings of artists alongside paintings and sculpture, as works in their own right. An entire exhibition might be about drawing. Do designer's drawings fit into this context? Are they worthy of inclusion in a museum?

Designers approach drawing in differing ways. Paul Smith, fashion designer, does not draw, but creates the starting point for his individual clothes with words in notebooks, carried with him constantly. Practising designer Dick Powell of Seymour Powell Design has produced a book looking particularly at presentation drawing: *Presentation Techniques,* published by Orbis in 1985. Objects designed by architects are an interesting subject area in their own right. The New York partnership Swid Powell has combined the drawing talents of architects from around the world with mass production techniques in tableware. Sketches and drawings for a range of picture frames, candlesticks, plates and bowls show the particular way in which individual architects have responded to a domestic product brief. The drawings in the exhibition *Design Process, Progress, Practice* tell us three things. They tell us about the design process, the working methods and creative style of the designer, and the finished product. But many do have an aesthetic and a presence beyond mere information, and they can stand alongside the drawings of artists. The contribution of designers to the history of drawing, which is also the history of visual perception, has been and will continue to be vital. Already there is a hierarchy of discipline; the drawings of fashion designers and architects are the acceptable face of design drawing, but it is time now that the drawings of product designers and engineers get the consideration and appreciation that they deserve.

Mono Racer, wash drawing

Winfried Scheuer

The cidental n Design

Achille Castiglioni uses existing images, gadgets, tools and examples of mechanical principles. They are passionately collected from a variety of sources, and serve as an inspirational library. He turned the tractor seat into a neat piece of domestic furniture, a car headlamp into an uplighter.

When, in 1475, Italian artist Piero della Francesca painted an ostrich egg floating over the Madonna's head, symbolising virgin birth, he unwittingly inspired a modern product which arrived on the market some five hundred and seventeen years later: a light fixture of unpretentious simplicity, called Brera, manufactured by the Italian company Flos, and designed by Castiglioni. Perhaps making use of the accidental is an essential skill of a good creative.

Mastering the accidental. When the dog bites.

Castiglioni was a pioneering user of the readymade, long before it became the avant-garde thing in the 1980s. He developed this Duchampian approach to product design further than any other designer.

Blackpool sports car producer TVR provides a wonderful example of design development, influenced more by bizarre incident than by inspiration. When company owner Peter Wheeler's dog, Ned, took a chunk out of the front of a foam design model of their Chimaera, the resulting missing piece was in due course turned into a styling feature, incorporating the indicator light and running across the whole of the front of the production car. The Chimaera has since become established as a particularly well-shaped example of sports car.

Another well-known British design evolved not exactly as planned by the designers. The Dualit toaster's well-known appearance is defined by an angled surface on one side. This was not at all what the London design consultancy had intended when proudly displaying the 1:1 presentation model at a meeting. Management felt strongly that it looked too big and insisted that the designers remove some volume. This resulted in the unique shape of the archetypal kitchen classic that we know today: an example of 'design by committee', that rather untypically led to a product-shape with profile and character. A rumour circulating in the design community, that a manager at Dualit had actually used an axe to chop a corner off the wooden design model, was not confirmed by the design office.

The TVR Chimaera

Then there is the wife of the chairman, a much feared but little mentioned influence on the design process. It was Richard Sapper who recalled how

the late 1950s Mercedes car acquired wings when a chairman turned up with his wife in the styling studio.

Her views resulted in an unashamedly American fin-detail being added to the chunky car's rear wings.

Damaged in transport

The Start chair produced by Capellini is a wonderful example of how the accidental can interfere with the design process and shape its outcome: Munich designer Konstantin Grcic sent a small-scale, soldered wire model to Italy which broke while in transit. This caused no problem for the Italian prototipisti, as Grcic discovered when he went to Italy to inspect the full scale prototype:

'The chair model was put together wrongly, but better than my original. The result was a rather daring construction with immense leverage at the front legs. Never would I have dared to do such a thing. But it functioned... and looked mega-cool ! I left it that way.'

Indeed, the metal construction of the chair is unusual. Rational engineering logic would have eliminated such a solution from the beginning. The designer controlling the design development accepted and exploited the accidental interference.

Start Chair by Konstantin Grcic for Capellini

Salami for breakfast

Nick Crosbie, a partner in London group Inflate, recalls:

'One Saturday I was having breakfast, looking at a pack of salami slices. And there it was!

Our concept for packaging the inflatables.When I rang up the packaging company they did not have gold, only silver. So we used silver.'

The result was a fresh and economical way of packaging PVC inflatables, making them perfectly suitable to be purchased as gift items with convincing 'aha' effect.

But it is not only maverick designers occupying scruffy East London warehouses who use such ad hoc principles.

A partner of respected consultancy Pentagram in West London, when purchasing a carton of orange juice, found his inspiration for packaging Italian shoes in a cultured way – his design brief at the time. The new Pentagram-designed shoe boxes were in due course produced by a juice carton manufacturer.

Clogged paint filters

The most spectacular case of the unplanned leading to a new product brief was triggered in 1978 when the filters clogged in the spray room of James Dyson's ball-barrow factory. Looking for a cure, Dyson came across the cyclonic principle, which, after a lengthy maturation process, led to Britain's fastest growing production company today, making bagless vacuum cleaners.

In a way history repeated itself for Dyson, as it was his unsatisfactory experience using a wheelbarrow when renovating his house that had led to his ball-barrow enterprise in the first place.

The Dyson saga, triggered by coincidental discovery, is perhaps comparable in impact with the case of the Pfizer scientists: in searching for a new heart medication they ended up with Viagra, a miracle drug unexpectedly fulfilling a long-term fantasy of mankind almost on a par with the fountain of youth – a product still to be developed.

Shoe box by Daniel Weil at Pentagram

A pregnant woman complains

In a remarkable example from the late 1970s, the brief for a highly successful design development was defined by coincidence. The pregnant wife of a Stuttgart design teacher lamented that she had no device to lean her body against while doing kitchenwork. Her complaints led to a brief given to local design students. Soon afterwards a prototype leaning device was put together. It was spotted in the design school's workshop by a visiting company consultant, who happened to know about forthcoming workplace legislation requiring employers to provide rest facilities for employees who stood for long periods.

Having benefited from two coincidences so far, the innovative student design was swiftly put into production and became a genuine bestseller, showering the two creators with royalties for decades to come. The popular saying 'the wish is the father of the thought' is borne out in this case, originally triggered by a pregnancy, but resulting in a far-reaching problem solution.

The accidental in perception

The way finished designs are perceived by the public is of course equally influenced by circumstance.

The design community might rhapsodise endlessly about its ability to master shapes and create the desirable in the eyes of the consumer. Frequently however the consumer reads the shape of products quite differently. In the past the shape of specific cars caused them to be referred to as 'the duck' or 'the beetle' by the man in the street. There was even a 'pregnant chair'. Here consumers have provided memorable names for products which the marketing departments could have been proud of had they created them in the first place.

The return of the Ford Edsel

The Ford Motor company experienced adverse perception when introducing their executive model Scorpio with its much lamented 'fish-mouth'. It received heavy criticism even before it was launched in 1995.

'The new Scorpio is without a question or shadow of doubt, the ugliest car ever made,' was handsome motoring journalist Jeremy Clarkson's damning comment. In due course it flopped and was discontinued four years later.

This had happened to Ford before, with the Edsel. The term 'Ford Edsel' has entered the everyday language of the design community. It means 'failure'.

Design tools shape outcome

The limitations of representational techniques used in design can shape results too, leading to what is known as 'the school of origami design'. The term was coined by Ford's former head of design Uwe Bahnsen when referring to Giorgetto Giugiaro's boxy car designs from the early 1980s. Rumours circulated in the design community that the Italian designer could not draw in perspective. Whether or not a shortcoming in his drawing skills did in fact generate such highly successful designs as the Volkswagen Golf Mark One or Fiat Panda, both have profoundly influenced an entire period of car design.

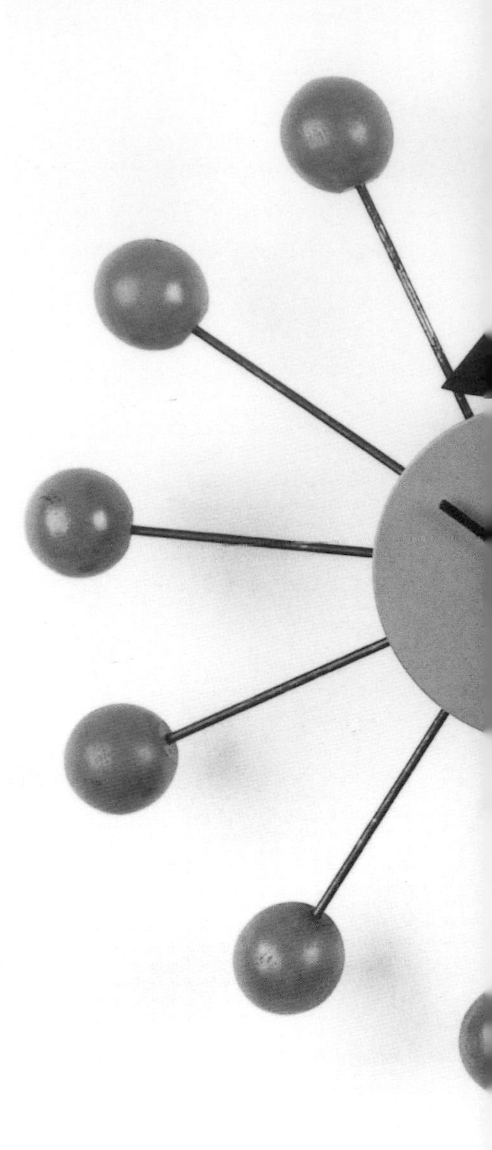

Ball Clock by George Nelson for Howard Miller Clock Company, 1947

Today industrial designers familiar with the latest CAD software programmes claim they can judge which programmes were used by looking at shapes of modern products such as telephones or computers.

'Taking a crack'

A well documented case of the randomly driven nature of the design process happened in 1947, when a true 1950s bestseller was created in the USA: the now highly collectable George Nelson 'ball clock', also known as the 'atomic clock'.

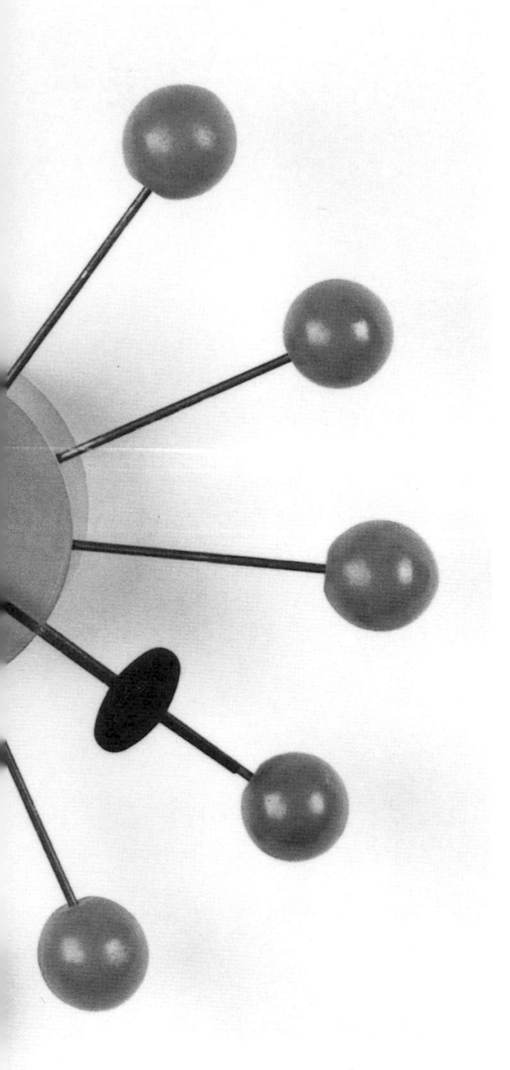

It succeeded in symbolising the spirit of an entire age. The case even involved the participation of three celebrities: Buckminster Fuller, Isamu Noguchi and George Nelson himself.

What Nelson recalls[1] of the events leading to the design is not what is normally imagined to be the design process: '...There was one night when the ball clock got developed, which was one of the really funny evenings ... everyone was taking a crack at this ... pushing each other aside and making scribbles. At some point we left, and we had too much to drink – and the next morning I came back, and here was this roll [of paper] and I and Irvine looked at it, and somewhere in this roll was the ball clock.

> I don't know until this day who cooked it up. I know it wasn't me...'

While frequent attempts are made to portray the creative process as highly structured and methodical, this is often clearly not the case, as the Nelson comments illustrate. 'Taking a crack', 'doodling' and 'cooking it up' are the exact terms he uses to describe the 'design development' of the ball clock.

Doodling: a method of exploiting the accidental

The ball clock's shape is easily imagined as an enlarged thumb sketch. The sketching involved, however, allows wider conclusions to be drawn. Sketching and doodling are more than the visualisation of the designer's own ideas, which have not matured or do not even exist the moment the pen starts moving on paper. 'Doodling', as Nelson calls it, is not necessarily a method of communicating with others, but a method the designer uses to communicate with himself. Doodles, unlike presentation drawings, are imprecise, incomplete, randomly driven, improvised and therefore open to all sorts of interpretations. They trigger variations and lead to new ideas in a playful, intuitive way. As with free jazz, the journey is the goal. Just as mountaineers can see 'a face' in a rock, doodles accidentally reveal shapes that were not intended in the first place.

Finally: Design Poker

Just as sketching can make use of the accidental in two dimensions, randomly generated shapes or combinations can be generated in three dimensions. The mid-eighties saw a boom in the objet-trouvé principle.

Pioneered perhaps by Daniel Weil who in 1981 stunned the public as well as his teachers

with a Duchamp-inspired degree show at the Royal College of Art, London, using stacked plastic funnels as lights as well as other ready-mades – a practice previously found in a less radical form in Castiglioni's work.

Three years later in a rare text, *The poet does not polish*[2], Jasper Morrison writes about a new type of designer: 'His office has no drawing board but is filled with these strangely significant objects which sooner or later he will invent a use for.' This was written in the year when the author/designer had turned a stack of terracotta flower pots into a table, today produced by the Italian company Capellini.

Morrison went further: 'Marcel Breuer, seeing a pair of bicycle handles, decided to make chairs using the same industrial process. The new world constructor ... decides to use them as they are and saves himself the trouble and expense of bending the tube.'

At the time, the supposedly 'found' was searched for systematically. Hardware shops and garden centres were plundered for ready-mades. The shopping trolley turned into a seat, the washing-machine drum became a cabinet, the bicycle handle a Morrison sidetable.

Little Beaver chair by Frank Gehry for Vitra, 1980

Telephone by Durrell Bishop, 1986

right:
Porca Miseria
exploding coffee set
chandelier by Ingo Maurer

In the hands of Andreas Brandolini, Morrison's colleague in Berlin at the time, the accidental element was shifted to the level of a design parameter. 'Design Poker' was born, and even patented, as a design tool – a generator of accidental combinations. With the help of playing cards which listed various activities, locations, and materials, these parameters could be brought together by chance. Design briefs were generated by shuffling the cards. Random combinations provided unique (and probably equally hopeless) product briefings for the 1980s student avant-garde.

The accidental as style

Durrell Bishop, a gifted Royal College of Art graduate, created a stunning telephone in 1986 by pouring plaster into a plastic bag and letting the contents dry. The shape was defined by gravity and by the random wrinkles of the wrapped plastic skin.

While the food industry had gone through elaborate procedures to make apples look perfectly identical, as if they had rolled off an assembly line, a small part of the 1980s design community worked in the other direction:

it perfected the imperfect, the rough and accidental.

The rewritten rules of the period suddenly allowed this, pushing a pluralism which included deconstructivist adaptations, randomly emerging details and a general lack of perfection. Perfection and rationalism, after all, were seen as key attributes of modernism.

The coffee set explodes

This period witnessed a virtual avalanche of the Duchampian, the found and the adapted. Following early examples in architecture, such as Sites' Best supermarkets with their ready-made crumbling brick walls, certain areas of design now accepted, even embraced, the randomly generated.

By the mid 1980s the randomly evolved and accidentally driven had become accepted as a style.

German light designer Ingo Maurer began to use bent wires, found plastic chicken feet and, more recently, a tea strainer turned halogen light. This development culminated in an exploding coffee set which turned into the Scherbengericht chandelier. Perhaps this product marked the end of a movement: a ludicrously expensive object, laboriously pieced together by hand.

[1]*George Nelson: The Design of Modern Design*, Stanley Abercrombie, MIT Press, 1995

[2]Kaufhaus des Ostens, catalogue, 1984

Roger Coleman

What desi

gn can do

If the world of the future will be full of older people, the last thing they will want is to be treated differently from everyone else. They will not want to consider themselves disabled, nor will they want gadgets to make up for the fact that they are perhaps less agile and dexterous than they were in their youth. Many of the supposed problems of old age are as much, if not more, to do with design than they are to do with the ageing process. There is a Gary Larson cartoon that shows a man being run down by a lorry with 'Age Truck' written on the side; as he lays in the road a bent old man with a walking stick and a tyre mark down his back comes up to him and says 'I see it got you too', and the caption reads, 'The Age Truck – you never see it coming'. The reality is rather different. Although we all find it difficult to accept the fact that we are growing older, the process is a very slow one, and we have plenty of time to adapt. We do not wake up one morning to find we are suddenly old, which means that we could quite easily adapt our homes, swap the bath for a shower, buy a car with power steering and assisted brakes, purchase new kitchen equipment, and generally arrange our lives and immediate surroundings to suit our changing abilities – or we could if enough things had been designed with older people in mind to make that possible.

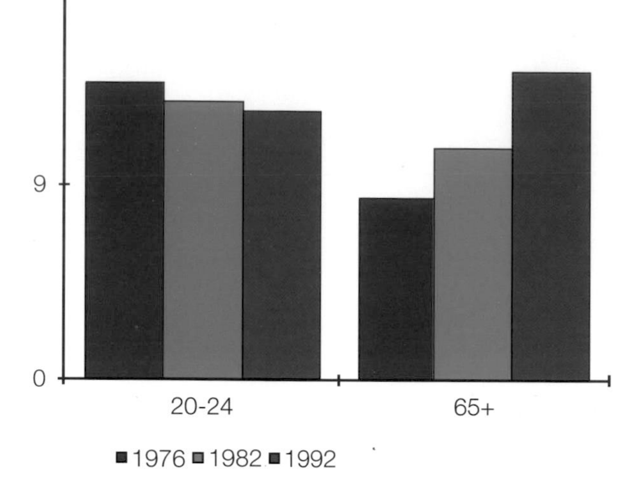

The time when the Age Truck really gets us is when we meet the first environmental barrier we cannot overcome – the pack we cannot open, the notice we cannot read – or the thoughtless remark that tells us someone else thinks we are old; that is when the Age Truck strikes and it can be a very painful moment. There is no elixir of youth, and no matter how much cosmetics manufacturers try to persuade us they can halt the process, and surgeons suggest they can reverse its effects by lifting and tucking our flesh, ageing is something we all have to live with. Since there are now so many older people, the current mismatch between them and so much of what is designed is rapidly becoming unacceptable. The obvious answer is to rethink the design of everyday objects and environments, but there is a deeper problem that stems from our fear of ageing. One of the reasons why we never prepare for or expect the Age Truck to come for us is exactly that fear. Few of us are comfortable with the idea of getting old, preferring to put it to the back of our minds.

Another reason is that we live in a consumer culture where youth is worshipped, where advertising and marketing are all aimed at younger people, and where few manufacturers are happy to have their products associated with older people. This tends to reinforce negative stereotypes of age and completes the vicious circle. Yet with the proportion of older people growing year by year and older people controlling an ever-increasing part of consumer spending, manufacturers ignore them at their peril. Once-lucrative youth markets are now contracting as an inevitable result of population ageing, which means that companies will have to compete harder to maintain their share of shrinking markets and even then will be losing sales volume. Those more far-sighted companies that begin to appreciate and value their older customers will benefit from more favourable trading conditions, with older people spending more money each year on goods and services which improve the quality of their lives.

This is where design has an important part to play. Better designed products can meet the changing needs of older people and still be attractive to younger consumers; they can open up new markets by offering older people independence and dignity and still attract younger people with good looks and functionality. Quality is a significant factor here; older people are experienced consumers who do not want to waste money, but will spend it on products that offer them the right mix of functionality, quality and appearance. Given the increased sales volume possible for those manufacturers that get it right, the price to the consumer can also be reasonable. Instead of paying a premium for good design, good design should ensure higher sales and more modest pricing: a virtuous circle from which producer and consumer both benefit.

A few years ago it was very difficult to find good examples of this new generation of age-friendly, multi-ability consumer products. Now the situation is changing rapidly. Good Grips in the USA, Bisterfeld und Weiss in Germany, and many other companies are beginning to fill this gap in the market with high-quality, superbly and professionally designed products, while other companies are beginning to innovate in selling to the older consumer, through catalogues and high street stores like Keep Able in the UK, and Kunde 50+, the new seniors' shop in Germany.

Extolling the virtues of Levi's heritage, this 1996 print campaign featured "original wearers", including Josephine, a 79 year-old teacher

Courtesy Levi Strauss/Nick Knight/BBH

Case study

Good Grips

Good Grips kitchen utensils have special handles designed to be comfortable and easy to use and hold. The basic range includes most standard items: knives, measuring spoons and cups, whisk, sieve, scissors, vegetable peeler, and is constantly being extended to cover all cooking activities with the addition of wooden spoons and utensils, ice-cream scoop, garlic crusher,

Good Grips garden tools

Good Grips kitchen brushes

Good Grips toilet brush and plunger

vegetable brush, apple-corer, and so on. A garden range is also being developed, beginning with fork, trowel and other small items. A key feature of the product is the large diameter handles, which are made from non-slip Santoprene rubber. These are easy to hold, soft to handle, and give better leverage in use. Each handle features patented soft spot grips on either side which provide extra friction and act as contact points.

The design of the handle

distributes the gripping force and by doing so minimises the amount of hand strength normally required. This allows safe and effective use of all utensils, and a comfortable, cushioned grip for everyone, regardless of age or ability. Among recent additions to the range is a kettle which combines ease of use with safety features and attractive modern styling. The elegant integral heat shield protects the user from accidental scalding, while the rubber handle is set low on the body to reduce wrist strain when pouring, insulates against heat and will not slip in wet hands. The spout cap locks open with a simple motion for easier pouring and filling, and the large lid is easy to remove yet seals tightly when in place.

Good Grips were designed by Smart Design of New York, and produced for Sam Farber by the OXO company (part of the US General Housewares Corporation, and no relation to OXO in the UK). Sam Farber's wife Betty developed arthritis which seriously restricted her enjoyment of cooking. Having already built up a good business wholesaling kitchen equipment Sam Farber felt this was a problem he could do something about. He invested some of the money earned from selling his original business in developing a completely new product: Good Grips. Sam's skills were in marketing and selling products, which meant he understood the value good design can add to a product, making the difference between success and failure. Believing he had a winning idea on his hands, he brought in a leading New York design company, Smart Design, to work on the project.

The result of this collaboration is a high quality, good looking, functional product range that works well and appeals to people of all ages. Top cooks use Good Grips, upmarket kitchen shops and major supermarket chains stock the range, and the volume of sales means that all the items are modestly priced. Outside the United States the range is handled by committed distributors like Jim Wilkinson Promotions in the UK. Jim Wilkinson has spent his life in the business of cookware and kitchenware and believes that the future lies in high quality products that work really well, of which the Good Grips range is a prime example. The very rapid expansion of sales in the UK bears witness to the market that is available if the product is right and its special features effectively promoted. All of which bears out the contention that many apparent disabilities, like the difficulties experienced by Betty Farber, can be minimised through good design that matches the functionality of products with the abilities of the widest range of users, and does so in a stylish, non-discriminatory way that can, with careful positioning, command a good market share.

Case Study

Age-friendly interiors

Bisterfeld und Weiss is a well known German manufacturer of quality furniture which has specialised in mainstream products, tables and chairs, in particular for the contract market. With an emphasis on wood-based materials and fine detailing, B+W furniture combines practicality with the warm tactile qualities of wood and fabric. With very little attractive yet ergonomically functional furniture available for older people, the company identified a clear need, and market opportunity, for furniture for the home and for more institutional settings. The company first developed an easy chair, with a foot rest, arms that fold down to make it easier to get in and out of, and a side panel-cum-pocket for books, needlework or other personal items. This chair preserves the material and high-quality detailing of the contract furniture, reinterpreting it in a more sedate and visually stable form, and including ergonomic features to improve comfort, especially for people who spend most of their day sitting in the same place, making it ideal for use in homes and institutional care settings.

The success and appropriateness of this product speak for themselves, but the company, and their designer, Arno Votteler, were aware of an equally important gap in the market, this time for furniture which functions well for older people but is thoroughly domestic in appearance and styling, and does away completely with the stigma associated with furniture designed specifically for the elderly and disabled. The overall concept was to produce a range which included all the elements needed to furnish a room – tables, chairs, cupboards – and make it possible to create an attractive personal environment, especially for people who live predominantly in one room, or in a small space. The range was

designed to bring functionality to the domestic environment, without compromising on appearance, and to bring the warmth and taste of the home into institutional settings and sheltered housing.

The product specification was developed on the basis of market research, consultation with end users and care professionals, and with attention given to manufacturing processes and volumes, quality and appropriateness of materials and detailing, and value for money. Design and development was carried out over a two year period, with professional advice being taken on ergonomic elements. All items were given practical tests in hospitals and other settings, and user-tested for functionality and acceptability. Styling and detailing were coordinated to produce a coherent range which offers a complete solution and convincing market proposition – a mix of durability, functionality, appearance and value that can form the basis for volume production and a good market share. The appearance of the furniture is restful which is important for older people, with attention given to the hygiene issues which are important for care managers. The intention was to achieve a formal unity and a clear and simple product language which could be integrated into a wide range of settings. Form, colour and material were carefully harmonised to communicate safety, stability and comfort, without compromising the objective of breaking the institutional mould.

Case study

Kunde 50 – the 50 plus shop

There are many arguments about the best way to market goods and services to older people or to people with disabilities. One of the crucial issues is the effect that separating out such products has on their acceptance. We know that technical aids are not generally liked because of their appearance and negative connotations, and the same argument is often used against the idea of retail outlets targeted at disabled or elderly people. While there is truth in this, the issue is more complex than it seems. In the past, aids and specialist products have had no presence on the high street, being sold by specialist medical suppliers with windows full of threatening equipment or available on trial at rehabilitation units or specialist centres like those run by the Disabled Living Foundation in the UK.

Recently however, spectacles have appeared in high street chain stores offering considerable choice at modest prices and with a matter -of-fact approach that has helped to make the wearing of glasses – the most ubiquitous of disability aids – part of everyday life, and the design of them an extension of the fashion industry. This opens up the possibility of other products previously seen as 'aids' making the transition from the margins to the mainstream where they are likely to be bought more readily, to improve in quality and reduce in price as a consequence of losing some of their medical connotations. It is almost bizarre that personal stereos, which damage hearing very effectively, are sought after, whereas hearing aids which are only another form of amplification equipment are not. Perhaps the young people of today will make the transition from Walkman to hearing aid with ease and style, and demand better products too. But whether or not there really is a market opportunity for high-

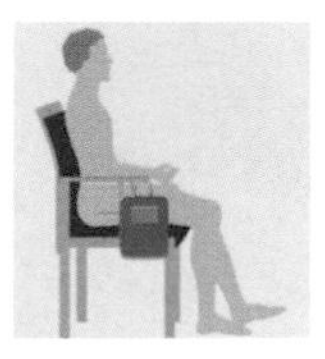

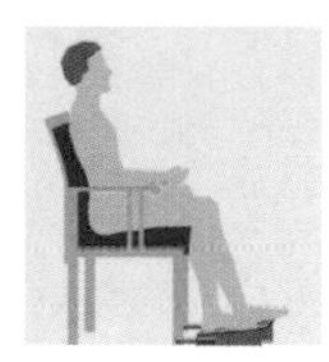

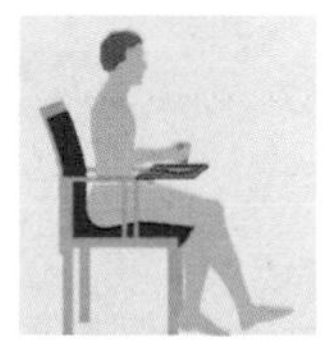

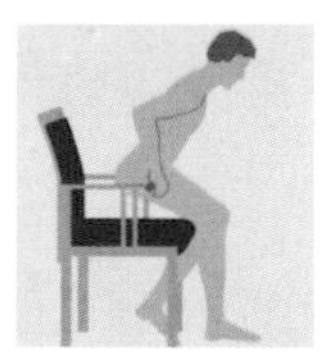

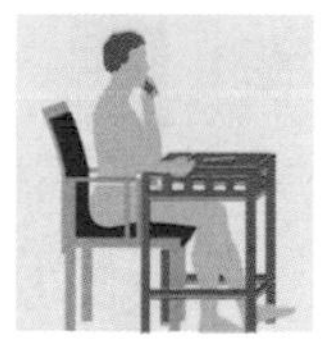

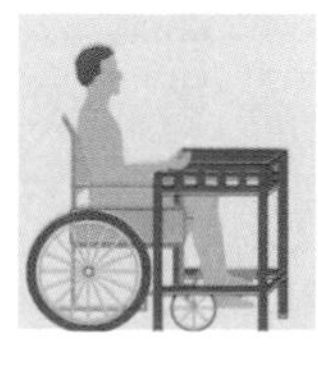

street shops catering for older people or people with disabilities remains to be seen, and will depend as much on careful marketing and positioning to ensure that people welcome their existence, as on the availability of the good-quality products such shops could stock.

In many ways this is a chicken and egg problem: without good products to sell, how can a shop look attractive enough to be profitable, and without an outlet for the goods, what incentive is there for manufacturers? However, there are now some very good products available, as we have already seen, and innovative retailers are trying to develop both mail order and high street outlets for them. This move is in its infancy and it is too early to really judge the potential, but clearly growing numbers of people need increased functionality and

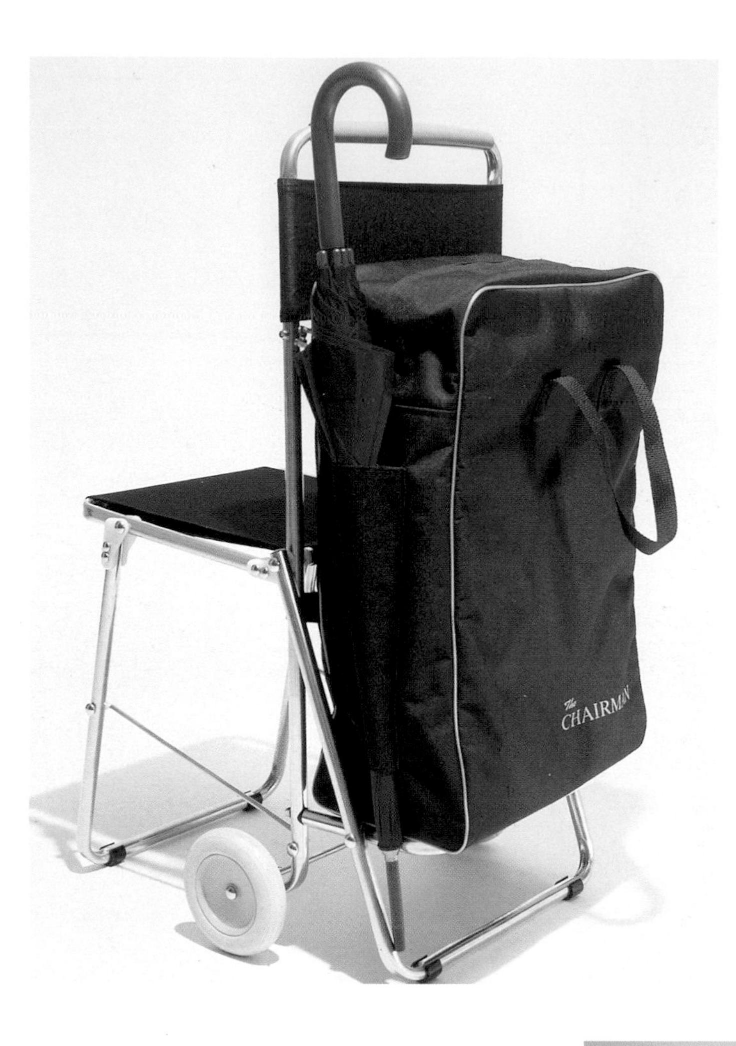

left: **Shopping Trolley with Folding Chair**
This shopping trolley combines a stable folding chair with a large, detachable bag with a zipper and pockets for purse, umbrella, etc.. It can carry up to 150 kg and is available in black, dark blue and dark red.

above: **Ball Pen**
An attractive pen that is easy to grip and hold, especially for people with arthritis.

right: **Large key telephone**
This large key phone combines user-friendliness with functionality, and includes a capacitor microphone for clarity, an inductive loop for hearing aids and tone or pulse dialling.

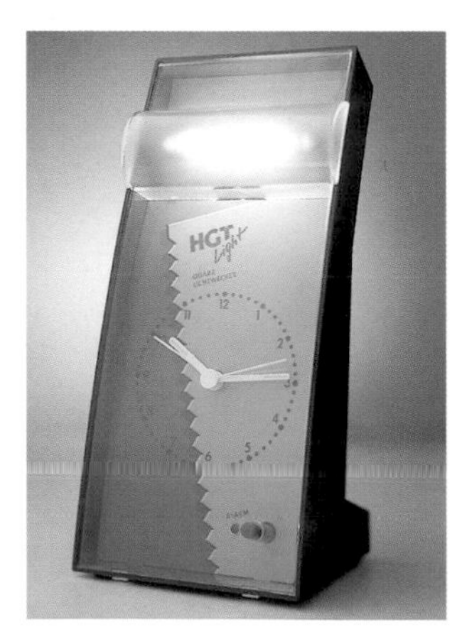

left; **Radio light alarm clock**
This well designed and intelligent alarm clock combines an alarm signal with a flashing light. Both can be switched off temporarily by a simple movement of the hand.

can benefit from the products that already exist, and the new ones that could be developed if the market were more easily identifiable. A sense of what is already available can be gained from a survey of some of the products offered by Kunde 50+ in Germany. These products address the needs of older people in various ways, with shopping trolleys in modern styling and materials, some with integral seats; games with pieces that are easy to handle; massage rollers and hand exercisers to maintain dexterity; telephones with large keys; radio alarms and lights that can be operated with a wave of the hand; spring loaded scissors and handy pocket key turners.

Shopping Trolley
This lightweight shopping trolley is available in red, beige and purple. It uses stylish materials similar to backpacks for young people. Kerbs and stairs are easy to negotiate, and despite its small size has a generous capacity.

Dice Game
Oversized dice are a pleasure to handle and easy to read.

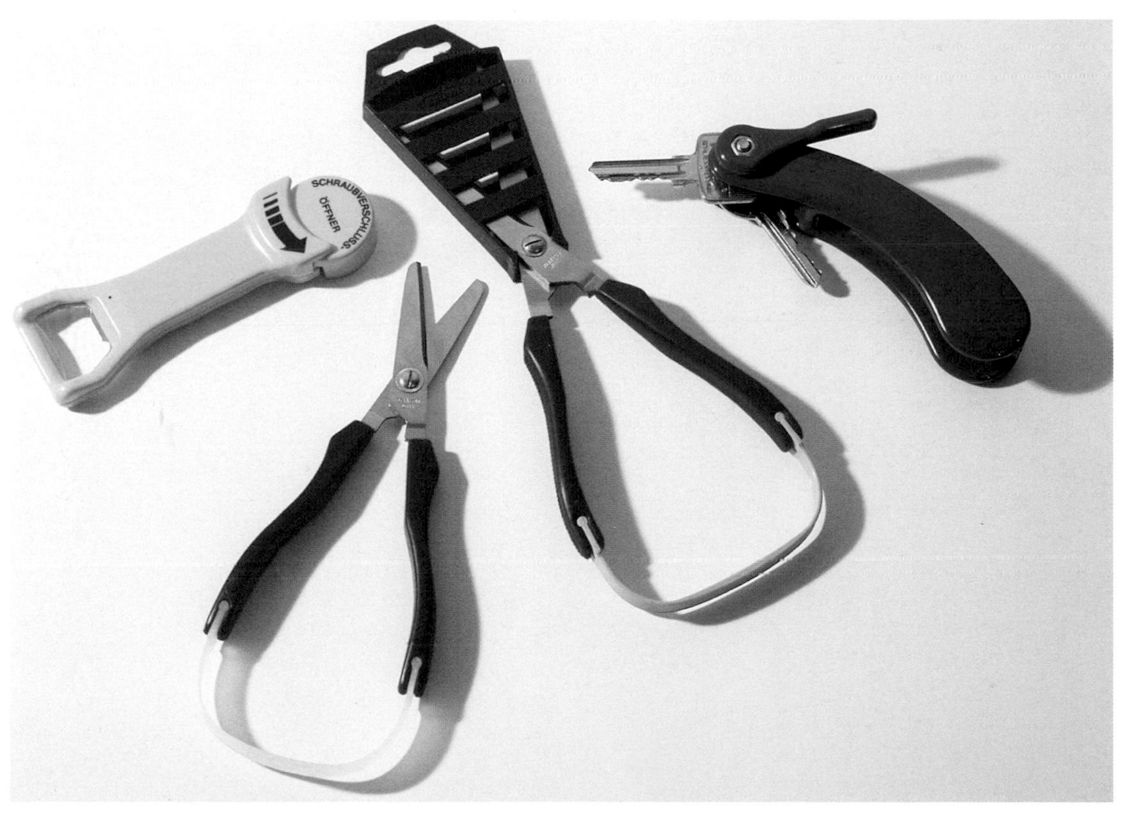

Key turning aid
Up to 3 keys can be screwed into the heavy plastic handle. Enhanced grip and leverage make turning the key easy.
Bottle opener
With this screw cap and crown cap opener, bottled drinks can be opened with ease.
Scissors
These scissors are spring loaded, which makes them easy to use, and come with a safety cover for storage.

Eric Kentley

De
without
Boat Buil
the

ign Designers: ing in Palk Bay

The difference between a good boat design and a bad one

can be the difference between life and death. Unsurprisingly, therefore, boatbuilders, whether planning a dugout canoe from a single log or a fibreglass mould, need to be able to reproduce successful designs. This may

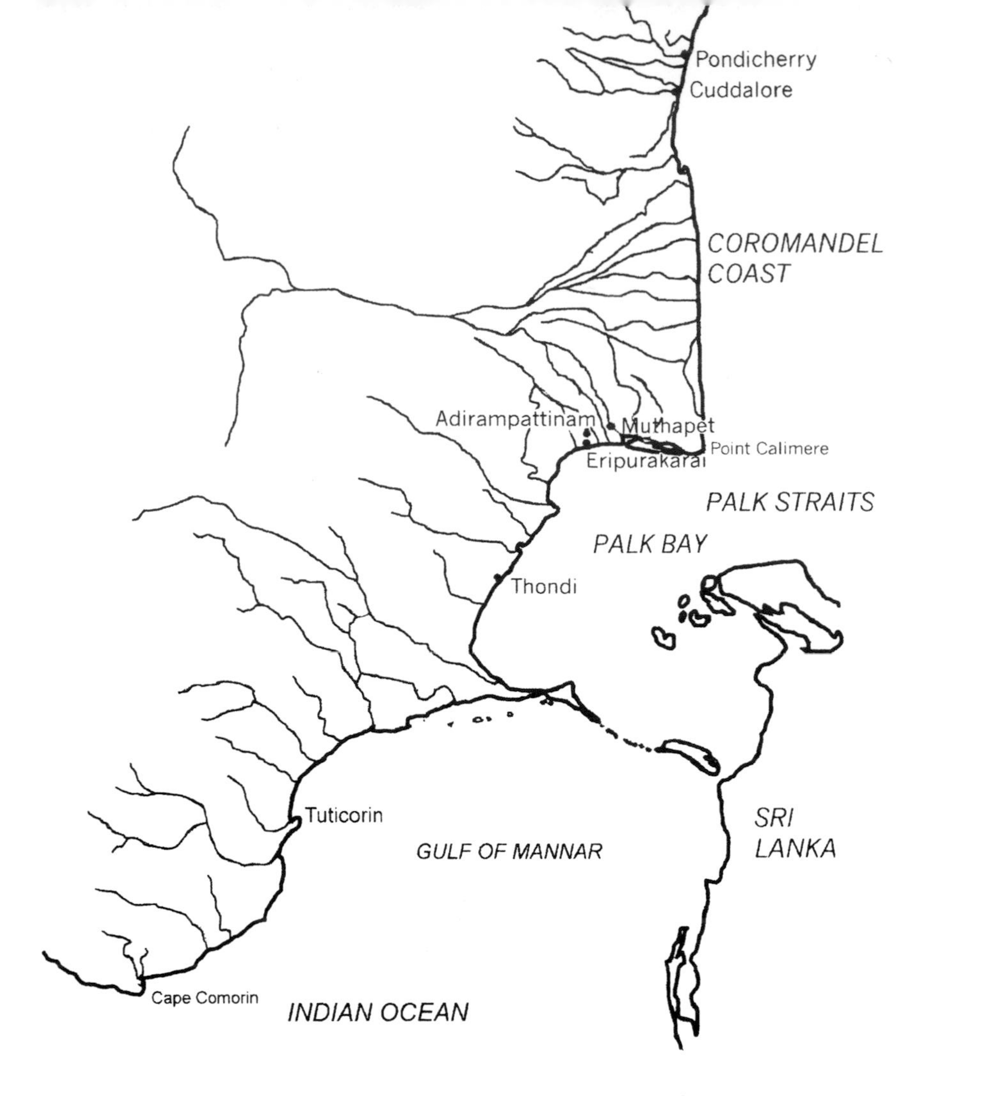

1 Southern Tamil Nadu (L. Blue)

2 *Thoni* at Tuticorin, without masts and deckhouse

involve recording information to create identical copies, or, more commonly, establishing a set of parameters within which a builder can vary the design. There is a huge variety of methods. Some builders create paper plans, some work from templates, some make models and others rely on a set of learnt formulae and years of experience. This chapter outlines one method that was found in the southern Indian state of Tamil Nadu in the late 1990s. It is a method which at that moment sat somewhere between craft design and industrial design.

Tamil Nadu has very active fishing and coastal trading industries and a wide range of vessels, from the log-raft *kattumarams* to steel-hulled trawlers. Within the state however there is a small group of boats which are designed by this singular method.

On the foreshore near the modern harbour in Tuticorin, once the pearl capital of the Indian Ocean but now just a minor port, there are a few boatyards still building large wooden vessels. Called *thoni*, they range up to 38 metres in length and the largest are capable of carrying 650 tons of cargo. Although they carry a mast and sail, they mainly rely on their big inboard engines for power. A similar vessel, the *kotia*, is built further north in the port of Cuddalore. The builders of these vessels, *mestri*, in Tuticorin and Cuddalore also build small fishing boats, a single-masted, motorised craft called the *vallam*.

Halfway between Tuticorin and Cuddalore, in the fishing villages of the Palk Bay from Tondi up to

3 Tuticorin *thoni* under construction

4 *Vallam* out of Tuticorin

Muthapet, there are dozens of small boatbuilding yards; some with just two boats on the stocks, others with as many as twenty-five in assembly at one time. The predominant boat being built here is the *vattai*, most of them just short of 14 metres in length but a few as small as five metres. In shape they are all very similar with a remarkably high bow which looks much more suited to a surf-beaten coast, such as that found in the Bay of Bengal, rather than the muddy shorelines from which they operate in the northern part of Palk Bay. In 1999 motorisation had made no real impact on the *vattai* and there may have been

5 *Vattai* sailing out of Muthapet. Note the balance board

as few as just two on the whole coast fitted with engines. Literally hundreds and hundreds of *vattai* sail out daily to fishing grounds in the bay. The large *vattai* are exceptional because, whereas fishing boats generally perform just one function, the *vattai* fishermen set nets and trawl for prawns on each trip. To trawl, they sling the net between the bow and the stern, hoist up to three sails and sail broadside to the wind. They are narrow boats in relation to their length and with the amount of canvas they set they would be quite unstable if it were not for a balance board laid across the boat on which crewmen and ballast can be placed to act as counterweights. The *vallam*, *thoni* and *kotia* have neither balance board and nor a high bow – what links these vessels with the *vattai* is not appearance but a common design method.

Figure 8 is a rectified construction drawing of a *vattai* at Eripurakarai in 1997 which shows the boat's structure. Essentially it is a skeleton of twenty-seven assemblies of timbers running across the boat frames—to which the planks are nailed. It is flat-bottomed with no keel and there is a long parallel-sided, and wall-sided, middle section (compare with the thoni under construction in Figure 3).

The *vattai* builders do not need anything as elaborate as a construction drawing like this to create the boat: all they draw are the outer shapes of the frames. The principles of designing a vattai are firstly to create a number of frames of exactly the same size and shape to form the central section of the boat. These are called the 'equal frames' and in the boat depicted in Figure 8 are the fifteen positioned from the seventh from the bow to the twenty- first. Secondly, a number of pairs of frames are designed to be erected forward and aft of the central section. These are known as the 'unequal frames'. On Figure 8 there are three pairs - the sixth and twenty-second from the bow, the fifth and twenty-third and the fourth and twenty-fourth. Other

6 *Vattai* near Thondi

7 *Vattai* scrieve board, with frame shapes drawn for two boats

vattai had four pairs and simply by adjusting the numbers of equal and unequal frames a certain amount of variation in shape can be achieved. The three frames in the bow and the three in the stern are not designed in the same way. Once the stem and stern posts, the equal and the unequal frames have been erected, the builders use battens to simulate the curve of the planks as they bend towards the posts and from these they trace the shapes of these six 'passive' frames.

The process of designing the equal and unequal frames begins with preparing what an English

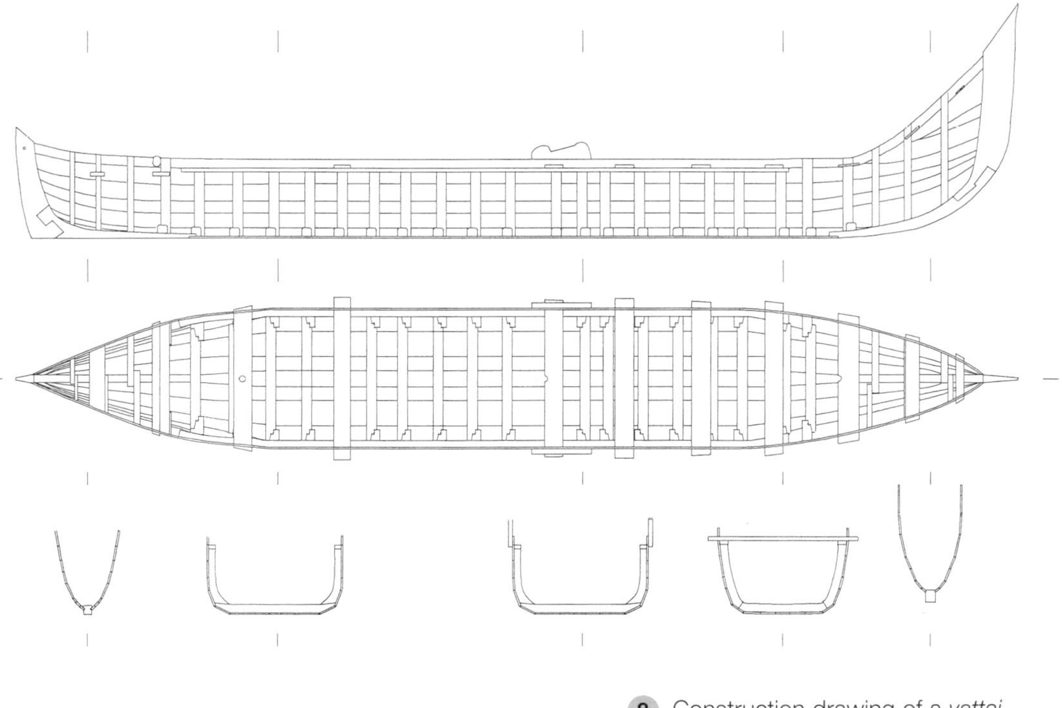

8 Construction drawing of a *vattai* measured at Eripurakarai

9 Scrieve board in action

boatbuilder would call a scrieve board: a few planks fastened together to make a horizontal surface on which the frame shapes can be drawn. On this board a rectangle is drawn, the length of which is equal to the width (beam) of the boat at its widest point and the width of the rectangle equals the boat's depth at the widest point. These dimensions can be adjusted to suit a client's specification for a boat deeper or shallower, beamier or narrower than another. The rectangle is bisected by a line which divides the beam into two halves, and then two further lines divide it into quarters. Finally, diagonal lines are drawn from the centre

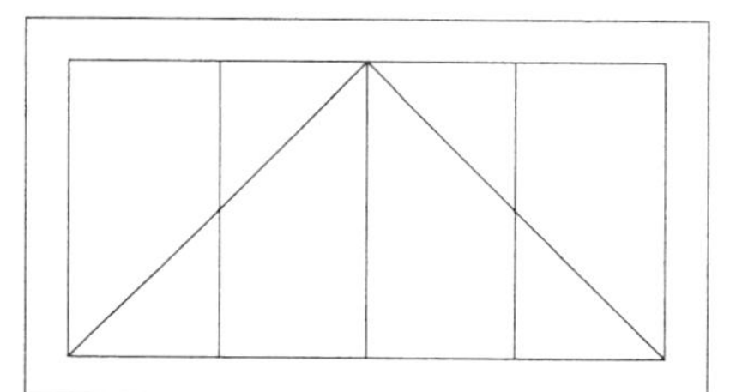

10 Diagram of scrieve board at the beginning of the design process

of the upper side of the rectangle to the lower corners, forming a shape shown in Figure 10.

The first step is now to define the shape of the boat's cross-section at the centre where the bottom meets the side - the turn of the bilge. The *vattai* builders simply measure a distance from the bottom corner of the rectangle along the diagonal - usually 4½ in. The shape of the equal frame can now be drawn by using a flexible batten (such as a bandsaw blade) as a spline to join the three points on the board: the top corner, the point on the diagonal and the centre of the lower line. From this a simple wooden mould can be made; and indeed once made it can be used again for all boats that require the same turn of bilge.

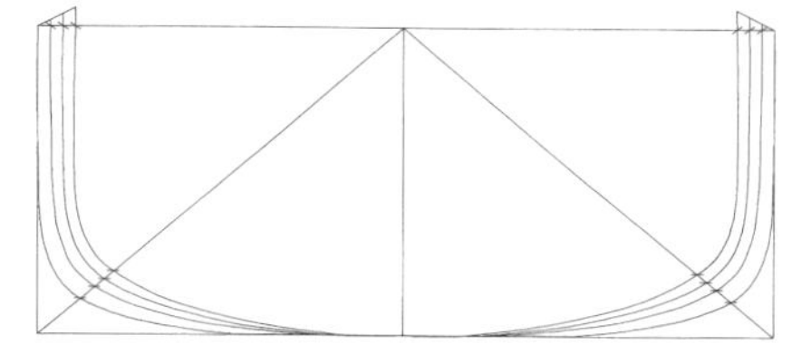

11 Diagram of frame shapes showing rise of sheer

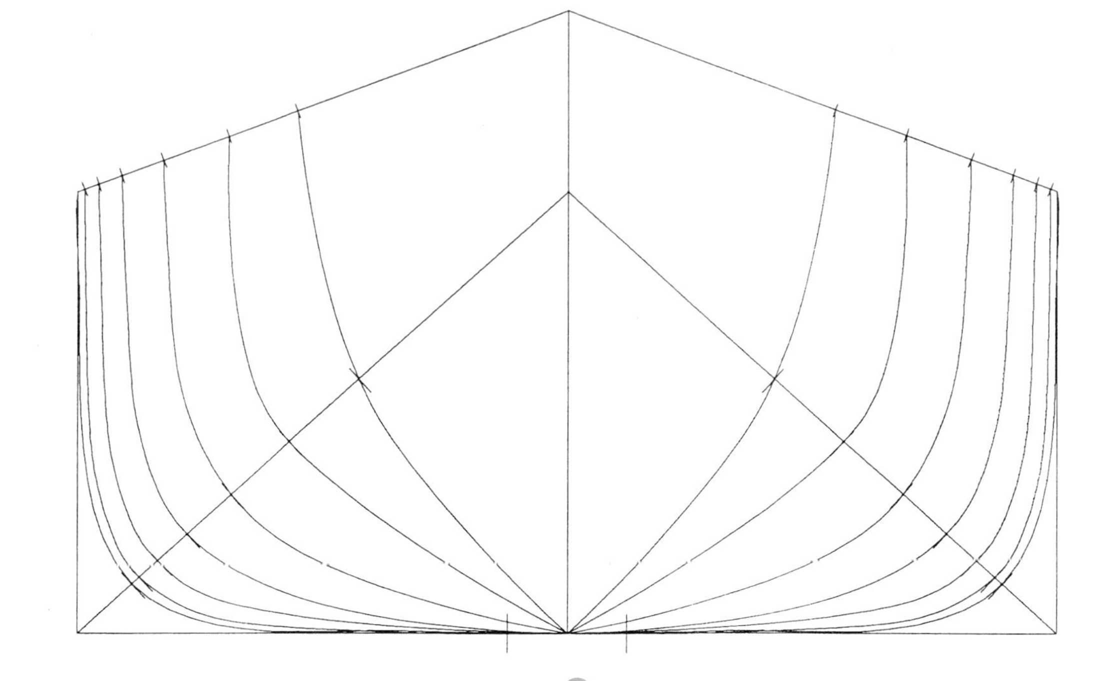

12 Diagram of *vallam* frame shapes on scrieve board

The shape on the scrieve board is the template to create all the equal frames, while the mould is used as an aid to draw the shape of the unequal frames, as shown in Figure **13**. On the board, further points are measured along the diagonal and along the top edge of the rectangle, representing the narrowing of the boat's beam (Figure **13** a). The mould is placed to draw a curve between the mark on the diagonal and the mark on the rectangle's top edge (Figure **13** b) then rotated to draw another curve between the mark on the diagonal and the centre of the bottom line (Figure **13** c). The resulting line is of course two separate curves, not a smooth single curve, but it is good enough for its purpose. Once all the unequal frame shapes are drawn on the board, they are then transferred to the timbers which will be cut into these shapes to make up the frames.

Thus, by the manipulation of a few measurements, a reasonably wide variety of *vattai* can be produced. The *vattai* drawn in Figure **8** has a flat sheerline (the shape of the top edge) for the entire length of its equal and unequal frames. However, a boat owner may ask for a rise of sheer. Figure **11** recreates the scrieve board to show how the boatbuilder achieves this simply by fixing the height of the last unequal frame at 1½" above the equal frames and extending a line down to define the height of the other unequal frames.

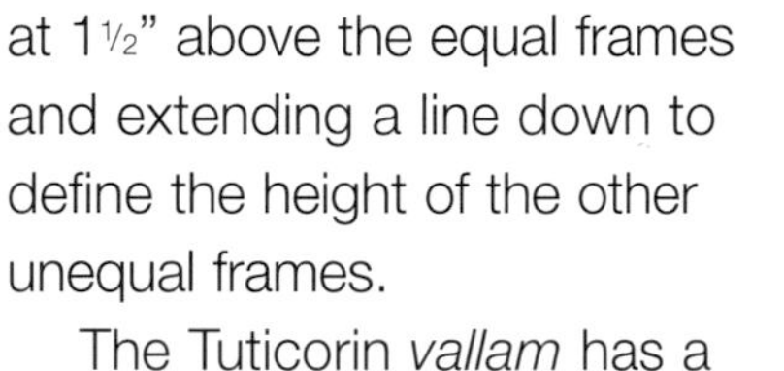

The Tuticorin *vallam* has a shorter midship section than the vattai and, although lacking the high bow, it has a gentle sheer along the boat. The builders of these boats use fewer equal and

13 Diagram showing how the scrieve board is used

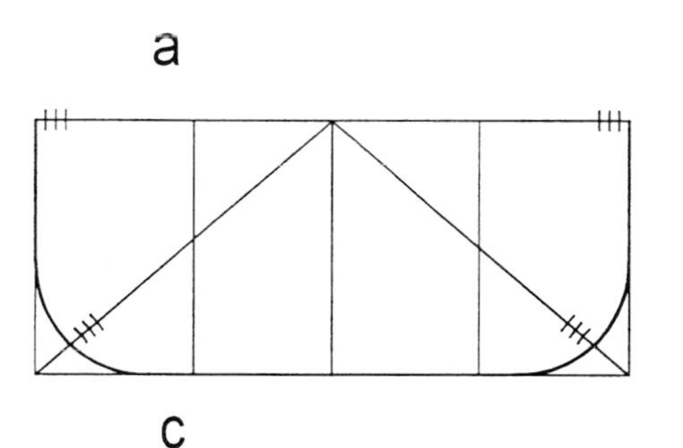

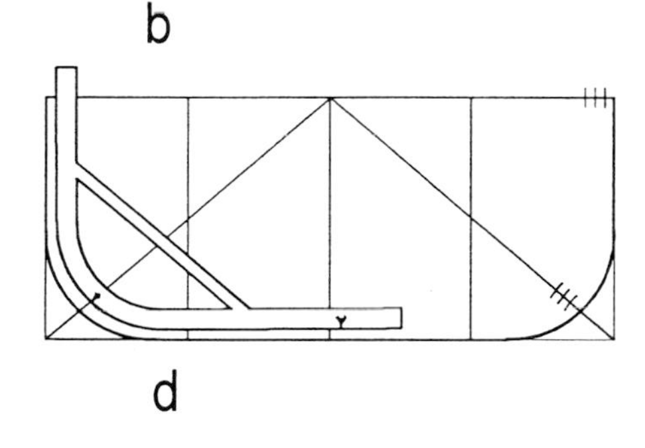

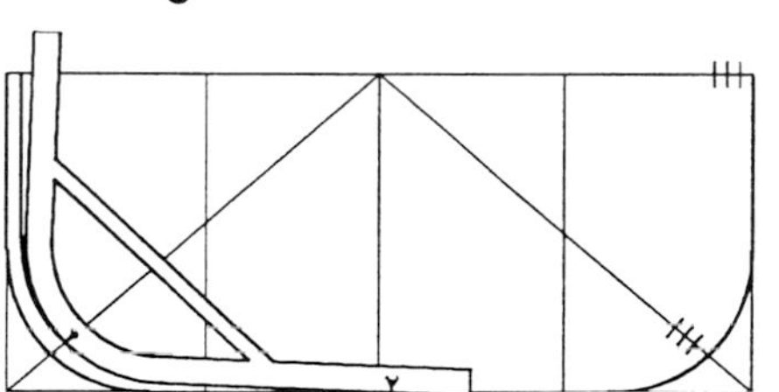

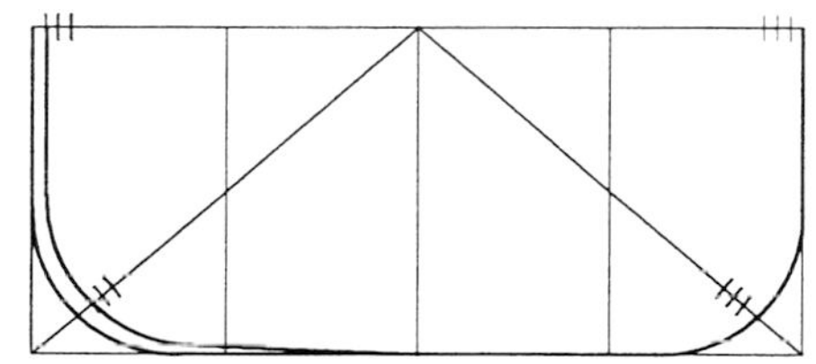

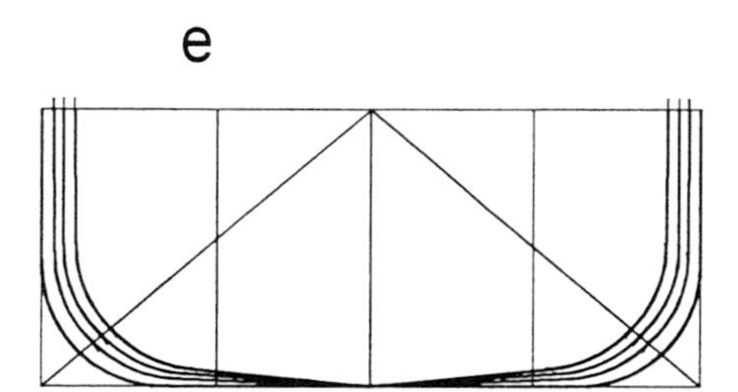

more unequal frames to achieve this shape but use a scrieve board in almost exactly the same fashion. The main differences are firstly that, instead of drawing a rectangle, the height of the boat at bow and stern is marked in the centre of the board and a diagonal line drawn between this point and the height amidships. Secondly, the *vallam* has a keel, unlike the *vattai* which is truly flat bottomed, and so the shapes of the frames are drawn on the scrieve board not to the centre but to the edge of the keel. Thirdly, the final unequal frame is of such a shape that it cannot be drawn with the mould and must be drawn on the scrieve board by eye.

Designing frames for the big thoni is a process more similar to that described for the *vattai* than that for the *vallam*. Here however the *mestri*, if he is not simply reproducing an exact replica, actually creates a scale plan at 1:16 on paper or card. He then measures off the positions where the frame shapes cross the diagonals and the distance between the top of the equal frame and each of the unequal frames and scales these up. The resulting table gives him all he needs to draw the frame shapes on his scrieve board, using a huge mould. Twenty-five equal and twelve pairs of unequal frames is a common combination for a *thoni*.

There are three reasons why this method is curious. The first is that the construction of these boats is not typical of Indian boatbuilding. Globally speaking, building boats with planks can be divided broadly into two principal methods. One either erects a skeleton of frames and nails planks to it to form a watertight covering –skeleton construction– or one makes a watertight shell by fastening planks together and then stiffens it by inserting frames or crossbeams—shell construction. The *vattai*, *vallam* and *thoni* are examples of skeleton construction,

but, except in boatyards producing vessels of Western designs, shell construction is the usual Indian method. An extreme example of shell construction are the surf boats of the east coast. The planks are sewn together with coir rope through pre-drilled holes and when construction is nearly complete a number of cross beams are fixed on the boat's top edge to hold the sides apart.

14 Mould used for building a *thoni*

15 Frameless surf boat on the Coromandel Coast

Shell construction is a very widespread technique, not confined to India alone. It is the traditional method of boatbuilding in northern Europe, where clinker planking, in which one plank overlaps another, is the most obvious indicator. Skeleton construction, usually with planking laid edge-to-edge – sometimes called carvel planking – is associated more with southern Europe where it is documented as existing in the fifteenth century but may date back to the thirteenth century or earlier. It was in ships built in this manner that the great voyages of exploration – of Da Gama, Magellan and Columbus were undertaken in the late fifteenth and early sixteenth centuries. By this time, the northern Europeans had seen the advantages of skeleton construction and carvel planking, with its ease of maintenance and repair. Indeed from the mid-fifteenth century onwards, this became the standard shipbuilding method throughout Europe, although the shell /clinker method is still in use for building small boats. If a similar 'evolution' occurred in the corner of southern India under discussion, it was adopted wholesale, for vessels big and small.

The second reason why the method is intriguing is that, although it is perhaps understandable that the sheer size of the frames on a vessel as large as the thoni require that they are physically plotted before they are cut, it is difficult to explain why the method is used on a vessel as simple as the *vattai*. Why does it need this method at all? With the exception of a ubiquitous mechanised fishing vessel built to a 1950s' European design, all other documented wooden fishing boats are built 'by eye'. This does not mean that the boatbuilder makes up the design as he goes along: builders work within a tradition producing near-identical craft through a combination of experience and a number of learnt controlling formulae or ratios, governing, for instance, the length of a boat to its beam. Boats of considerable size can be built in this way. Dhows of India's west coast and the Arabian Sea of 30 metres were built seemingly without as formal a design system as the *vattai* which are half their length. The differences in shape between the equal and unequal frames are so small (see Figures 11 and 13) that it is difficult to believe that an experienced boat-builder could not shape these frames 'by eye'. On the *vallam*, however, the differences between the frame shapes are greater and might therefore justify the method more strongly, yet, as noted above, the final unequal frame has to be drawn 'by eye'!

The uniqueness of the method of building boats makes it inconceivable that the practices described for the construction of the *vattai*, *vallam* and *thoni* are not variations on a single method. As practices on large boats are more likely to filter down to small boats than the other way round, one can imagine a possible diffusion where the method was first used on the *thoni*, then used by *thoni* builders making *vallam*, adopted by other *vallam* makers, who then applied it to the *vattai*; finally it was adopted by builders who only made *vattai*. This is of course impossible to prove either way, but even if it could be, there remains the question: why is this untypical practice found here at all? There is a possibility that it is a local technique but, because it does not seem to be known elsewhere and occurs on a stretch of the coast which has over the centuries seen a wide range of foreign ships (and, possibly, shipbuilders), it seems more probable that it had its origins abroad.

The Portuguese reached this coast in the early sixteenth century, and established forts, as did the Dutch, Danish, French and British who followed them over the next three centuries, so there is no shortage of possible sources of the method. Although there is no system in any of these countries which exactly mirrors that described above, it does bear a resemblance to a method used to build schooners in Bahia, Brazil, described by John Sarsfield in the mid-1980s, which in its turn is thought to be related to earlier European systems of design, Portugal being the obvious point of origin. These schooners are more curvaceous than the Indian vessels but nevertheless have a system of equal and unequal frames. Again a mould is made of the same shape as the equal frame but in conjunction with a marked board, as shown in Figure 16. Intriguingly, there is a close similarity between the *thoni* builders and the Bahai schooner builders in the name they call themselves: *mestri* in India, *maestri* in Brazil. The differences between the two methods are sufficiently large to suggest that they are derived from some now-lost common design method. The Indian method in particular may be just a relic of a more elaborate method. It is tantalising to speculate that it could be a relic of the method used to design the ships of the great European navigators, a process about which we know very little.

There is at least one clue that the system now in use in India may once have been more elaborate. On the scrieve boards illustrated in Figures 7 and 10 there are two vertical lines dividing the hull into quarters. These lines are completely superfluous: they play no role in designing the frames whatsoever. Yet they survive (at least on some *vattai* scrieve boards) and one can only conclude that they must have had a purpose at some point.

The third curious aspect of the method is its incompleteness. It is a set of rules and procedures which allow one to create part of the boat, but not all. The design method fixes only the shape of the frames: it does not help with any other part of the vessel, for example with the height and curve of the *vattai's* stempost.

The *vattai* builder must shape this 'by eye',

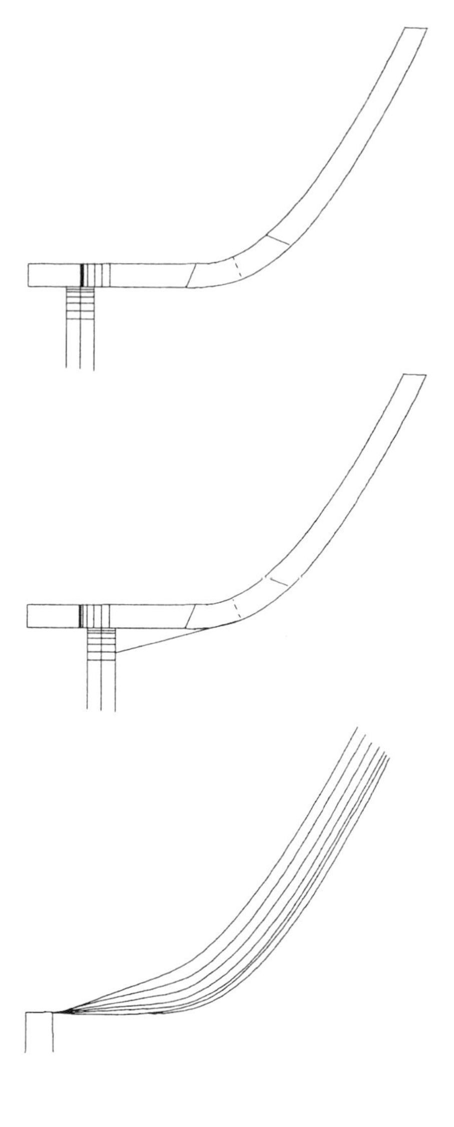

16 Bahia design method

Top
the shape of the equal frames

Middle
aligning the mould with a "rising board" to draw the fifth unequal frame.

Bottom
the equal and six unequal frames drawn out (after Sarsfield)

with a mixture of experience and mental formulae. It is worth noting that the shape of the post is not fixed by a long tradition or by a functional requirement. Photographs taken earlier this century show *vattai* with much lower stems. The high bow is simply modern styling.

Again, although the stemposts of the *vallam* and *thoni* are straight, they are raked and the angle of the rake is set by a learnt formula, not through a drawn design. The same is true of the Bahia schooners: the method does not extend beyond the frame shapes. But although it may be a limited technique, it does have several advantages. It allows a fair measure of variation in size and shape to be introduced simply by altering the number of equal and unequal frames. For the *thoni* it may do little more than give formal control over the shaping of the frames. For the *vallam* and the *vattai* possibly its greatest advantage is that it aids mass production. Large quantities of frames can be produced from a single design operation on the scrieve board, enough to make several boats at once. This is perhaps why one rarely sees a yard with a single boat under construction. But most importantly the mould is a data bank of learnt knowledge about successful frame shapes and documents experimentation.

If one regards the history of mass production as an evolution from craft process to industrial process, this method lies in the hinterland between the two. It still has a strong element of designing 'by eye' but it is not a huge leap from the curves on the scrieve board to a naval architect's plan. A seventeenth-century European draughtsman would use a pair of compasses to achieve a two-sweep section, which the *vattai* builder achieves with his mould, but the result is similar. Indeed, the *thoni* builders draw a plan very similar in function to a European ship's body plan. But the evolution of processes need not go in only one direction. Those redundant vertical lines on the scrieve board may be an indicator that in the Palk Bay, the techniques of industrial process are being adapted for a craft process.

Research on these boats was undertaken by Professor S. McGrail, Dr L. Blue, C. Palmer and myself, funded by the Society for South Asian Studies. Fuller accounts of the building of these boats appears in *South Asian Studies*, volumes 14 and 16.

Perry King

Desig

T

n Process: he Future

What is the process of design going to be in the future?

The future is all around us but it is very difficult to identify. We only recognise it by the changes that occur when the things that we are used to and know alter or disappear and new things and ideas take their place. Then, of course, it is too late. The present has caught up and a new future waits to be identified.

Recognising this may make us wiser but it is of little help in attempting to foresee the future unless we can identify a pattern in past changes which indicates a pattern in the changes that may be possible in the future.

If we look at the most distant past in search of this pattern, we can see that, for countless generations, men and women, the forefathers of today's designers, have worked to decide the shape, colour, form and utility of the everyday objects and tools that other people use daily. These nets or baskets, tables or chairs, pots or pans, jewels or clothes, knives or forks, were designed and made and then bought and sold, used or neglected, borrowed, stolen, treasured or thrown away in just the same way as we treat the tools and objects in our homes today.

The tools and objects that survive from these distant people (distant in time and sometimes geographically) which can be admired in museums and collections are, of course, the pieces that have been most treasured, valued enough to ensure that they were handed down from generation to generation and even then only if they were made of the most durable of materials. We know very little of the necklaces in coloured seeds and shells, of the hats and capes made of hummingbird feathers, of the banners and covers in linen or silk of long-forgotten peoples, but the pieces that have survived often touch us in unexpected ways. We feel that we can recognise in them some of the qualities and values of the people who produced and used them. We perceive them as objects that are an expression of the civilisation that produced them. What we discern is the 'content' the designer gave to them as he designed them.

Almost always the people who designed these objects were the people who made them, each one slightly different from the other, and then sold them on to people they knew.

© Feather cloak, Hawaii, 18th century
British Museum

They shared their values and knew and understood each other's way of life.

Often they made them for an individual customer, to order, with the specific characteristics that the customer requested.

This clear relationship, which survived for thousands of years, was swept aside, destroyed, in a few years of revolution by the development of what is called in our school books the Industrial Revolution.

Like all revolutions this one brought huge changes and numerous new opportunities. For our purposes perhaps we could say that the most important of these changes was that the designer no longer made the objects he or she designed. They were produced identically in very large numbers to be bought by large numbers of people whose location and way of life were, for the most part, unknown to the designer.

The designer had become a professional: the designer we know today; an expert in materials, space, form, colour and people's reaction to them; a professional working in a complex series of interrelationships, for a large or small organisation, itself under pressure from competitors and shareholders to increase market share, decrease costs and provide ever better margins. The designer was no longer a craftsman making the objects he designed by hand with simple tools who considered his craft skills to posess value in themselves and whose responsibilities were confined to himself, his family and perhaps his guild.

New opportunities for design were created, new fields developed as people recognised that products had to be advertised so that they could be desired. They needed packaging for protection and consumer recognition, then they had to be transported and finally sold in the very competitive

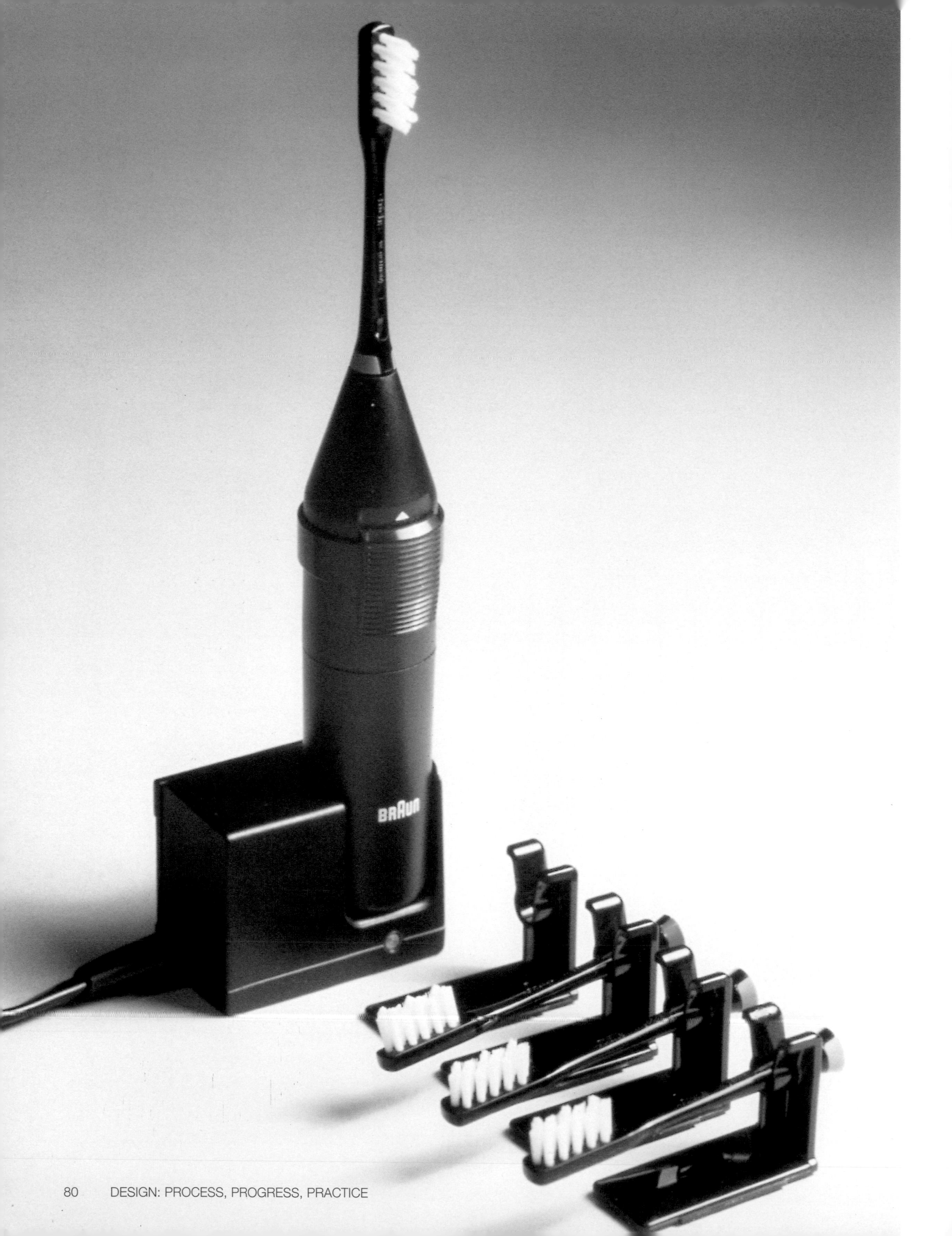
BRAUN

environment of ever more specialised retail shops, themselves in ever increasing competition.

These pressures completely changed the relationship between the designer and the person who used his designs and, even more important, they changed the relationship between the object and the people who bought and used it. Even though people were faced with a variety of products, produced in hitherto unseen quantities, the range of choice in some ways became more limited. Each product was exactly the same and yours was just the same as your neighbour's. There were many to choose from and

you could have them any colour you wanted as long as it was black.

Braun electric toothbrush ZB1/D1, 1978
Robert Oberheim and Reinhold Weiss

Designers faced with great energy and optimism the problems generated by their distance from the users of the objects they designed and by the fact that they were designing objects that were identical for a host of people who were anything but identical. They were designing for individuals, each one different from the other: different in age, ambition, culture, desire, habit, vice and virtue.

Back in the 1940s and 1950s designers felt that design was going to change the world. It had social relevance; it was good for you, like cod liver oil. A new generation of industrialists set out to show that industry could benefit from demonstrating that it had responsibilities to workers, to customers and to the environment: responsibilities which went beyond the hard, single-minded logic of maximum profit. Industry learnt that quality brings success in competition and that good design is part of the recipe.

Over the years some of this optimism was lost. There was an industrial logic which seemed to indicate that the largest market was the best market. As 'good taste' distinguished one from the masses, so vulgarity was seen by some, in an odd association of ideas, to guarantee the mass market – in industry just as on the television; a sort of lowest common denominator, deplored by everyone but accepted as inevitable.

As the years passed, there was an increasing dissatisfaction with the role of design perceived by both the more attentive designer and by those few observers – critics, journalists and academics – who dedicated time to considering the role and future of the profession. It was felt that design risked becoming a mere marketing tool whose only function was to increase sales: a profession without ideas. Only a limited minority of designers were able to demonstrate that a better product will sell well, to take the risk of independent thought, and they were considered to be designing for an intellectual elite in some way divorced from the realities of the industrial world.

Just as crisis seemed inevitable a new revolution occurred which has radically changed our perception of the profession. It occurred just in time, just when it no longer seemed possible to believe in design as one of the major artistic expressions of the century (as I firmly believe it is), one that has touched more people and involved greater investments than many more obvious expressions of our age.

This new revolution was the introduction and development of information technology, a phenomenon as dramatic as the revolution which had characterised the previous two hundred years, and with similarly far-reaching effects. Even the way designers work has been transformed. Graphic designers who used to work with pencils, brushes, paper, card and cow-gum, now design on the screen. Designers of objects or spaces who used to draw with pens on tracing paper and who had to make models to see their designs in the round, now elaborate their ideas using virtual three-dimensional models which exist only in their computers. But these developments, important as they undoubtedly are, have not yet radically changed the designer's thought process. The designer's work is still essentially the same as it was twenty years ago. The real significance of the new technology is the effect it is having, or will have, on the way products are made, on the way they are communicated, on the way they are sold. These are the changes that will make the designer think in a new and different way. These

Apple Macintosh M001, mid-1980s

new technologies may, if we are lucky, provide us with the discipline that designers in the past enjoyed until they stopped being the makers of their objects.

The implications of all this are only just beginning to become evident, but I am sure we are on the threshold of a whole new language. There is a poetry that can be expressed through the new technology and this may well be the poetry of the future. It is a most exciting moment for us because as designers we can help to dictate the grammar of this language as we use it.

The end of the second millennium has, as we have seen, brought changes which we can only begin to assess and only begin to appreciate. Like the last revolution this one is opening new doors and closing others, bringing new opportunities and limitations. In the same way that the last revolution brought new fields of design and new forms of expression so has this one: fruit of the technology itself. Above all it has broken the shackle that had taken our profession to the point of crisis that I described. It has created the need for a new kind of designer.

above: Advertisement for Olivetti Standard Typewriter, 1920s

Over the years it has been necessary to reconsider several of the keystone ideas that seemed to be central to the profession. One example was 'functionalism'. For years functionalism was the justification for all sorts of unfriendly objects in our homes. Functionalism, which was good, was contrasted with 'styling', which was not good. Then, fortunately, the famous phrase 'form follows function' came to be perceived as inadequate unless 'function' was enlarged to include emotional satisfaction and pleasure. Later a new phrase came into vogue: 'problem solving'. It too became another excuse for limited thinking. Everyone will agree that problem solving is a very necessary task but it is a simple one compared with the much more urgent and important task of identifying the problem in the first place. The new designers need to become innovators; not so much problem solvers as identifiers of problems that must be solved. This is a necessary point of transition towards a new definition of the aims of design, more in tune with the electronic age that we now live in.

If in the past design was to do with the transformation of materials now it is to do with

above: Advertisement for Olivetti Valentine, 1970, Milton Glaser Lords Gallery, London

the transformation of ideas.

Certainly this new freedom will require ever higher levels of professionalism on the part of designers who will be working for industries that, having accepted the logic of the new technologies, will find that the stakes are typically higher, the pay-off slower and the penalties for error greater than they were in the past.

In order to understand those future changes in the design process that can be foreseen in the pattern of change we have examined, it is necessary to talk a little about the new designers and about content, motive and creativity. Thinking habits will have to change just as they did at the start of the industrial revolution. Very little room will remain for the designer who does not feel at home with and understand the new developments, who is unable to use them and to exploit them in his or her creative activity. There will be greater complexity, more collaboration and teamwork. At the same time the new designers will recognise that, to take advantage of new opportunities, they must ensure that the quality and value of products they design are as high as they can make them: products, interiors or services

Olivetti Valentine portable typewriter, 1970
designed by Ettore Sottsass Jr. and Perry King

whose content is both rich and satisfying and which are, just as we saw in those artefacts in the museum, an expression of our culture of which we can be proud.

The increased complexity that we have seen will mean that the new designer will be aware that his every action is political, on the grand scale and on the small scale: the choice of a production technique that will display concern for ecological matters or the choice of one project over another that cannot be made without expressing an opinion about its use and place in society. The new designer will have to define his or her own model of an ideal world or risk being, as someone said, a fool giving shape to other people's ideas. The new designer will be concerned with connections, realising that today's actions are a product of our yesterdays and will influence our tomorrows. He or she, aware of connections and with their private model of an ideal world, will know that design is not just about the form of an object, it is also about the way things are used, how they are communicated, the way they are organised and produced. The new technologies are already transforming production techniques and management methods, making it possible to achieve efficient production of small batches of products with a high technological content. These are already allowing manufacturers of products as complex as automobiles to consider making them to measure, to satisfy an individual customer's desire for personal choice.

New communication techniques make it possible to interact with the customer, to study his or her habits, wishes and desires on an almost individual basis and to satisfy them in a way that has not been possible since designers/craftsmen made single products for people they knew. Designers will be able to renew the relationship they once had with the users of the things they design: not just consumer categories, but real people, with ideas, hopes, ambitions and fears; a relationship that they lost with the Industrial Revolution. In this way they can help to ensure that the relationship between the object and its user is as rich and as meaningful as possible.

Industry needs independent thinkers and the new designer will be a man or woman of independent thought. The best architecture is produced by architects with their own scale of values which are, of course, necessarily different from those of the property developer. In the same way the best design will be done by designers who have their own values and do not necessarily share the values of the industrialist whose responsibility is to make a return on shareholders' capital. The new designer will realise that industry is a vehicle of expression, to be nurtured and cultivated, but will also realise that industry has values that are different from the values of the designer. This independence is the very reason that industry will employ the new designer – to question and propose new solutions.

The new designer will concentrate on content, not on the repetition of calligraphic gestures or signs, and will be aware that design is not just the creation of sculptural objects but is giving form to collective values in which everyone, or at least a large number of people, can recognise themselves. It is responding to needs that people do not yet know they have.

Hong Kong and Shanghai Banking Corporation Headquarters, 1979-85
Foster and Partners

HILTON

Bill Moggridge and

A New

Tim Brown

Challenge for Design

Faced with the complex problems of designing modern technology-based products, services and spaces, it is tempting to return to the basic values of aesthetic contribution. Design has, however, always been concerned with

the whole experience of interacting with the product, service or space.

Working with complex products, networked services and interactive spaces has taught us how to design machine behaviours, to understand more about cognitive psychology, anthropology and sustainability.

It has made us more skilful at designing experiences, gestures and rituals. It has helped us to create appropriate expressions that have meaning and value over time.

In a complicated modern world, with technology coming from every direction, we need to remember emotions. Even for the design of complex products, services and spaces, the aesthetic value will come first from the beauty that we see, the shape, proportion, texture, colour and finish. As we spend time with things, our relationship with them extends into an interactive experience, so that we are affected by expressive qualities of gesture and ritual, and by what we feel and hear, perhaps even taste and smell.

Many people think of product design as the creation of the form and shape of everyday objects, an idea that is reinforced by the display of products on pedestals in museums. We think that this is a misleading notion. Products, services and environments must always be designed in a broad context that considers the whole experience of use and interaction. Rather than thinking just about visual aesthetics,

we need to be creative in the design of expressions and behaviours.

Take for example a very simple object like a champagne glass. If you think of it as a static object, you can design the shape, the proportion of the base to the stem, the material thickness and flow. To design the static object successfully, you must also think about the requirements for manufacture, and the demands of market and distribution. These aspects on their own offer interesting challenges, but the opportunity to create an aesthetic experience comes into its own when you design for the whole experience. Does the stem give the tips of your fingers a little tingle of pleasure? Does the aroma of the wine float towards you as you lift the glass? Does the rim feel just right against your lips? Does the sound of the material ring true as you touch your glass against another?

Compare the champagne glass to a cell phone. They are both hand-held objects that you lift to your face, both intimate, and both designed to help you do something. The design of the shape of the cell phone poses similar challenges to those of the glass, and can be authored by an individual designer. The object as a whole is likely to be designed by a team that includes industrial design, interaction design, ergonomics, mechanical engineering, hardware and software engineering. The experience of using the phone will also depend on the design of the service and the supporting infrastructure. What is it like to navigate around the software to make the call? What messages does the system give to the user? How is each transaction supported? You hope not to notice the transition between cells. You do not notice whether satellite or land-line is being used for long distance. You just assume that the conversation will be clear and uninterrupted. Creating a beautiful cell phone is similar to creating a beautiful champagne glass. Designing an engaging expression for the glass can be intuitive. For the cell phone a host of design contributions from people from many different backgrounds will be needed.

To influence the whole experience successfully, we need to know how to design for the way we speak, listen, find the right person to speak to, make connections, leave messages, know what a dial tone and a ring sound like. We need to be able to rely on an infrastructure that is smoothly engineered for seamless connectivity, so that the technology is not noticeable. We need to be able to create an instrument that is small and light but also robust and reliable. It will be crammed with chips, circuitry, display, battery and so on. The complexity of this combination of opportunities and challenges is impossible for a single designer to grasp, even the most 'renaissance' person. Now we need a renaissance team, made up of people from lots of different backgrounds, dedicated to creating experiences and behaviours for objects and interactions and infrastructures. The people in the team need to trust each other to let their work overlap. They need to thrive on confusion, and to be willing to experiment all the time with who does what and how.

SOME IDEAS ABOUT PROCESS

The challenge of designing experiences and behaviours for complex technological systems needs to be met with new ideas about design process: ideas which build on the traditional strengths of design (conceptualisation and visualisation) and enrich them with new human- and technology-focused approaches. At IDEO we have steadily moved away from a sequential idea of design process towards a set of values which contribute to a rich design and innovation culture. These values provide a framework within which chaos, risk, experimentation, innovation and vision can thrive:

TREAT LIFE AS AN EXPERIMENT by constantly exploring new ideas through projects. Projects provide a structure for design and innovation with clear goals and criteria for success.

SIMPLY BEING MULTI-DISCIPLINARY IS NOT ENOUGH if we want to achieve visionary products and services instead of grey compromise. It is important to be smart about creating and sustaining groups of energetic, opinionated people from diverse disciplines and cultural backgrounds. At the same

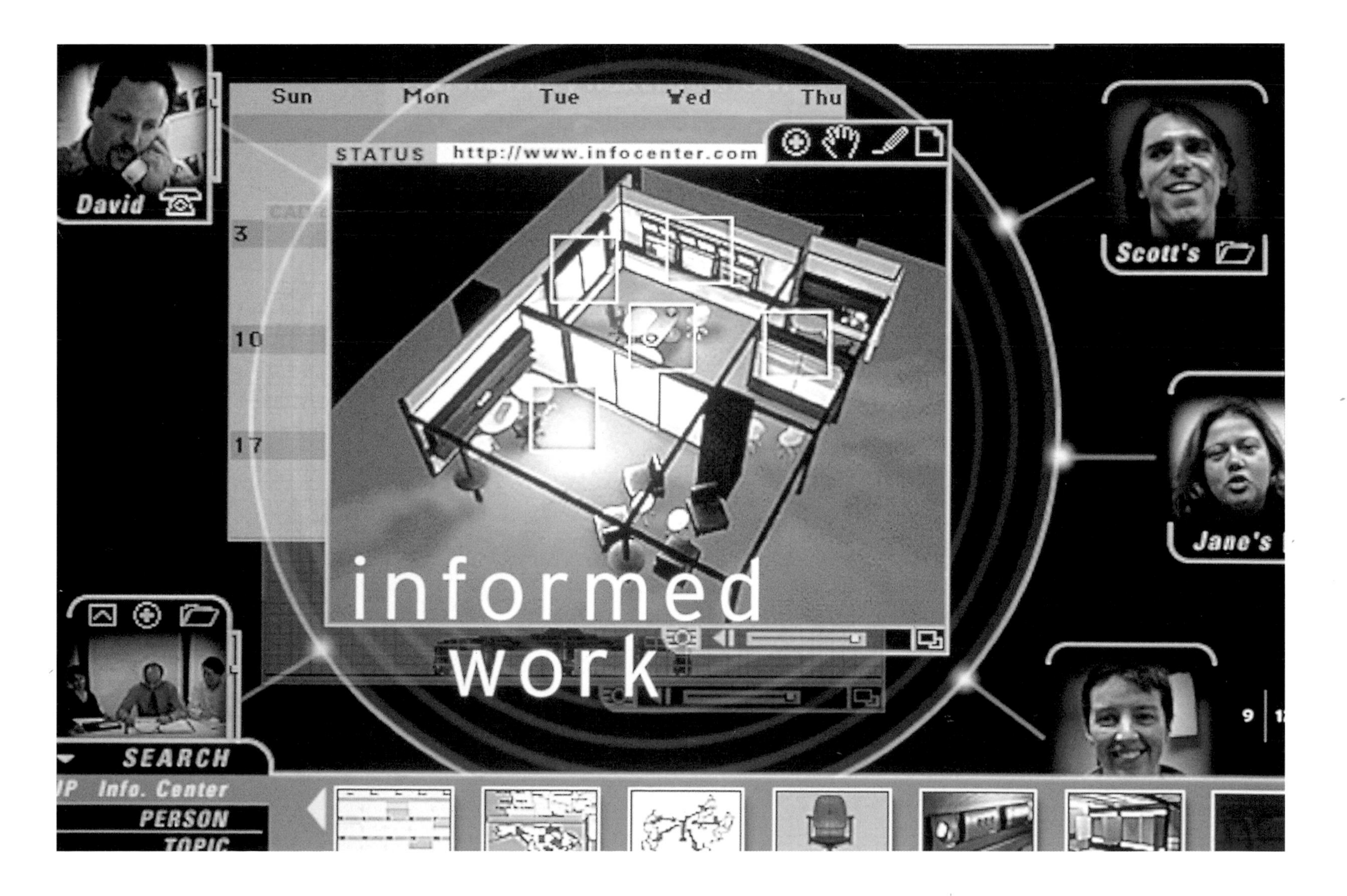

time, these teams need to have external goals on which all can agree wholeheartedly. These might be to satisfy certain user needs and desires or to achieve particular business objectives.

DESIGN THROUGH OBSERVATION of people, what they do and where they do it. It is by the careful study of the world around us, and how individuals interact with it, that we gain an understanding of what people really need and inspiration for what

they might want. Techniques ranging from the simple discipline of always observing and recording personal experiences to sophisticated programmes of user research carried out by teams of psychologists and anthropologists generate invaluable insights and ideas.

STEPPING INTO THE SHOES OF OTHERS means never forgetting that we are designing for people other than ourselves. Do not leave ideas of user focus to the early research stages of a project. It is too easy to fall back into the trap of designers creating products that are right for designers and yet we are responsible for developing ideas that are appropriate for both sexes, all ages, cultures and social environments. Hypothetical characters, based on knowledge and understanding gained from user research, can be used to populate storyboards and scenarios that become the environment for exploring and communicating ideas of interaction, experience and behaviour. Techniques ranging from simple sketch illustrations to video and computer animation help create rich and compelling narrative visualisations.

RISK A LITTLE, GAIN A LOT. Failing quickly and often through rapid prototyping and user testing is the quickest way to get innovations out into the world. The biggest mistake design teams make is to get too precious about the design process. It is far more useful to learn today with a prototype which is only eighty per cent right than wait until next week for that last twenty per cent. The challenge of designing complex smart behaviours has resulted in the emergence of the new discipline of 'user experience prototyping'. This brings together CAD based prototyping techniques with new low-cost electronics and software simulation platforms to allow designers and engineers quickly to simulate and prototype product behaviours with off-the-shelf technology. This is invaluable when we are attempting to design and understand new product archetypes such as digital cameras or electronic books.

ALLOW SERENDIPITY TO PLAY ITS PART. Remember that the best learning and some of the most inspired ideas happen away from your desk. We need a constant reinjection of ideas and inspiration by getting out into new situations and environments.

"SPACE IS THE LAST FRONTIER". Creativity is difficult to sustain in dull, soulless environments where team members cannot easily interact and naturally move from one activity to another. We need constant stimulus around us in the form of technologies, materials, objects, images. We need to be able to hold an impassioned brainstorming session at one moment and then retreat to reflect and refine our ideas at the next before we move on to build our first quick prototype. Project teams need to be able to create spaces where they can work together and display all the historical content of the project. They also need technologies such as e-mail, Internet, video conferencing and multi-media to support the development and communication of ideas.

CASE STUDIES

The following case studies are examples of our attempts to apply these ideas of design culture to the challenge of designing behaviours for products and services, ranging from the future of the information age to simple everyday objects.

The first two examples are about being connected: connected listening and connected learning. As an infrastructure the Internet is revolutionary. Suddenly it is possible to connect every device to any other device, and so create new uses and services for people in a community unrestrained by place and distance. We need to think about the way the product or service is represented on the web, so that the experience of being connected through the Internet helps and supports the whole experience.

The second pair of examples are about the impact that digital technology is having in areas with an established tradition: listening to the radio and taking photographs. Here the impact of technology need not be noticed if the value that is gained supports the traditional value.

An interactive keyboard makes music more accessible for children. An interactive space helps people to work in teams with the information that they need, including those who cannot be there in person. Both examples celebrate the overlap between real and virtual worlds, so that behaviours and expressions are represented seamlessly in electronic and physical embodiments.

Our last two examples are unencumbered by the realities of market need and business success, exploring experiences for their own sake: the ritual of eating chocolate, and a feather lamp that delicately combines light and motion. The chocolates are expressing ideas about taste and feel as well as appearance and aesthetics. The expressiveness of the light seems to hypnotise you and keep you spellbound indefinitely.

01 Connected listening

Net Audio for Audible is like an Internet Walkman for the spoken word. Download spoken books or radio excerpts, grab your player and just press 'play'. It sends a radio signal so you can throw it in your car and listen through the car radio, or carry it with a portable radio, or plug in earphones to listen directly.

There are new challenges in designing this kind of connected information product. How does the website help you to browse through the library of spoken books and radio programmes? Is it easy to download from the computer? What does a digital audio player look like? Can you see how to use the controls? Here is an unusual chance to set a precedent, as this is the first of an emerging category. The design contains the familiar controls from tape players, in a nautilus shape reminiscent of the human ear

02 Connected learning

The StudyPro computer for NetSchools has an infrared link to connect children to the teacher in the classroom, to each other, to the school server, and to the Internet as a whole. They can browse and search for information, or send messages and work back and forth. The design has a magnesium case with rubber corner bumpers, creating a rugged but friendly form. The floating screen absorbs shock, so that it can be dropped without harm, and the keyboard will survive a spilled drink.

This is still a general purpose computer rather than an information appliance, but it draws its power from being connected. The challenge was to design it for the rough and tumble of life at school and home. Those curvy bumpers express a friendly smile as well as protecting the corners.

03 Digital Radio

This exploration for the BBC examines the opportunities that can arise from new digital radio transmission technology, and demonstrates them as scenarios of use, showing the potential to content providers and radio manufacturers. One scenario shows a radio that is shared by everyone in the family; another shows a personal radio that can learn about its owner; a third shows a series of special purpose radios used by one person in different situations.

Radio is a strong auditory medium, allowing the imagination to roam in the visual realm, painting vivid images to support the sound picture. Visible radio needs to be separated from the stream of sound, rather than being integrated with it like television. Digital radio can be used to make your choices visible, to help you know what is on and to find your way around. It can add new services like games or audience participation, but it should be designed with a polite deference to the tradition of radio, from wireless to digital audio broadcasting.

www.school

3 | 12

02

04 Digital moment

The interaction architecture for digital cameras and other imaging products and services makes manipulating digital images easy and intuitive, and allows the camera user to concentrate on pictures and not process.

A camera is a good example of an information appliance. Just a few years ago, a camera was a mechanical and optical instrument with a chemical film. Little by little the computer chips invaded. First it was automatic exposure, then auto-focus, and red-eye removal; now digital memory is replacing film. Though we still think of it as a camera, dedicated simply to the task of capturing images, it is not just a camera anymore. It's a camera, an album, and a way of editing and choosing. Somehow the design expression has to support all of these things. For Kodak the challenge is to create an interactive experience that supports the brand and the feeling of the right 'Kodak moment'.

05 Interactive keyboard

The orange, yellow and blue buttons on this interactive keyboard for Yamaha are coded to the selection of tunes and rhythms, and presented in instrument groups that are indicated by icons, so that children can experiment with and enjoy sounds without needing any skill with the piano keys. This can lead naturally into learning to play the keyboard.

There is a delicate balance to be achieved here: how to invite kids to experiment without destroying the inherent qualities of a musical instrument? Somehow the experience has to be both easy and challenging at the same time. The shape is like a pillow that protects the piano keys and contains the bubbling music, so that the object invites play. The traditional keyboard demands patience and skill to learn, but the synthesised sounds and music are made easy to access by the colour coding and grouping. Projects like this need teams of contributors with strong points of view: the musician, the industrial designer, and the interaction designer.

05

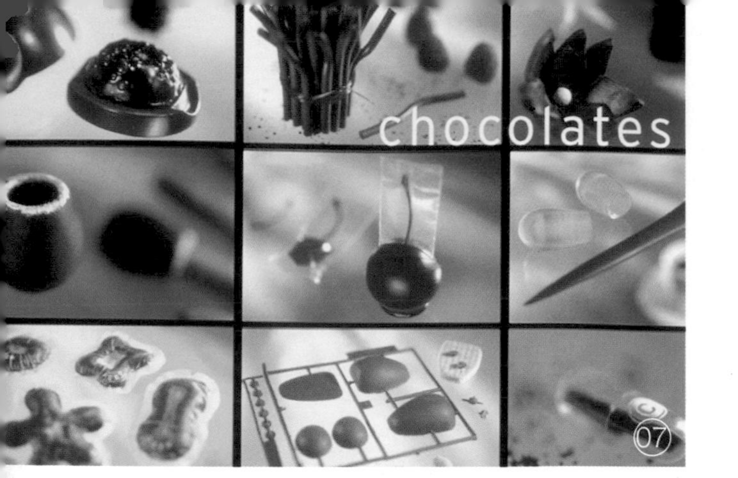

06 Interactive space

People want to work together in a space that helps them to access information fluently, and connects them to others who are far away. Networks allow people to work from home, or contribute to teamwork without being with the other people physically. This is making the office more of a social place, improved for collaboration and knowledge transfer. Media-rich spaces create a more seamless integration of physical and virtual. This collaborative environment for Steelcase allows team members to manipulate both the information content and physical characteristics of the space. The space becomes the surface on which information can be displayed, whether electronically or with traditional media.

The room is becoming a computer and the computer is becoming a room. This merging of physical and virtual space is exciting, but at the same time we want to be able to move fluently between information that is represented electronically and physically; for example between a projected display and a whiteboard. The designs of real and virtual information can be separate but linked.

07 Expressive tastes

The unique qualities of chocolate inspired a group of IDEO designers to search for new ways of both manufacturing and eating, and resulted in a collection with emphasis on ritual, delight, enquiry and surprise. One example is a kit that you can assemble yourself: lick and stick, then eat everything including the frame. If you don't like chocolate, choose the gel capsule with the chocolate inside. It will dissolve gradually in your stomach, postponing the effect of the caffeine and avoiding the taste of the chocolate. Try the coffee experience: a chocolate spear seals a hard candy filled with liqueur. Stir your coffee with it, so that the chocolate melts, making liqueur coffee and leaving chocolate for you to eat.

The idea of designing chocolates reminds us that there is potential to design for all five senses. We are used to designing to please the eye, and designing the sound, and the feel. Here is a chance for a richer sensuality as we also design for taste and smell.

08 Expressive lamp

Light, shadow, motion, and reflection; the feather lamp forms an environment through the behaviour of light and the gentle motion of the cast shadow, integrating high technology carbon fibre material with eggshell and feather. A carbon fibre rod extends vertically from the supporting base. A horizontal rod is balanced across the top, with a halogen lamp at the end, half enclosed by a cast form made of eggshells. The counterbalance is formed by a third rod that positions the feather of a dove just above the lamp. As the feather approaches, the convection current from the light source wafts it gently upward, casting a varying shadow on the ceiling above. The gently expanding and contracting shadow soothes with a hypnotic delicacy.

light
light
12 | 12

THE DUALIT TO

ASTER RANGE

Lesley Butterworth

A toaster belongs in a kitchen, but as a domestic appliance, and an electric one, it is a relative newcomer to the worktop. Kitchen worktop space is valuable territory. A toaster has to jostle for position with a variety of other products: juicers, bread bins, kettles, coffee-makers, mug stands and roll-dispensers, or it risks being relegated to the ignominy of the kitchen cupboard.

A kitchen reflects its immediate environment: a commercial kitchen caters for the eating requirements in a school, factory or restaurant; a domestic kitchen is a place for living and entertaining in, as well as for the preparation of food.

Prior to the Industrial Revolution, home and the workplace were often one and the same. The idea of the home as a private and personal space was unusual. The household of the Middle Ages was often a place of business and before the seventeenth century a house rarely had interior doors.

The period of prosperity after the Industrial Revolution led to increased consumer spending, encouraging mass production for mass consumption. There was also a growing interest in the home and in the idea of 'homemaking'. This gave rise to a variety of publications about the science and management of domestic work. To complement this research a growing range of domestic appliances came onto the market. To begin with a lack of steady power presented problems. Steam engines were too large for domestic appliances. Gas and electricity were introduced. Electricity was seen as cleaner and safer and soon became the main source of power to the home. Once installed it could be used for a growing range of appliances.

By 1920 a strong consumer market for domestic appliances had already been established, and over the following decade the output of the industry was to triple. Once an area had been connected to the National Grid, door to door salesmen would follow offering new products for new consumers. Fans, irons and vacuum cleaners were the most popular appliances, closely followed by toasters, but only once customers had been convinced that their toast would not taste of electricity.

During the first half of the twentieth century many electrical engineering companies moved from the industrial into the domestic market. Their success depended on the amount of money they could invest in the development of a mass production system. Domestic appliances such as vacuum cleaners and toasters were advertised as means to entice servants into employment, or as labour-saving devices for the house wife with no domestic servant.

Since the Second World War the rise in consumer demand has

escalated in parallel with the consumption of electricity and the sophistication of products. When domestic appliances were first introduced little attempt was made to create a specific image for them. The fact that they were new was enough of a selling point, and many early appliances looked like small industrial machines. Gradually companies began to use designers, often on a freelance basis, to create a visual identity for their products. As the century progressed, style and fashion moved into the kitchen, and appliances had to respond to these changes. During the 1970s a popular kitchen style combined stripped pine and flowers. This was followed by a more high-tech look in the 1980s, and then by 1990s minimalism. Toasters have followed suit. Russell Hobbs, for example, produced an 'Honesty' toaster for a 'rustic' kitchen, later covering it with a matt black finish as a different market developed.

The inventor of the Dualit toaster, Max Gort-Barten, was born in 1914. He studied engineering and worked in radio intelligence and with the Ministry of Defence in aircraft production.

left
The first Dualit toaster

previous page
The Dualit Combi (polished)

Warehouse:
Raw material awaits production

After the war he went on to found a small engineering company in Camberwell, London, where his first product was a double-element electric fire with parabolic reflectors called the Dual-Light. It was this product that gave his company its name. The Dual-Light was followed by a cocktail/milk shaker and a metal fire draught shield.

In 1947 the company started work on the product range that was to become their greatest success. The Commercial Automatic Electric Toaster and the Electric Flip-Over Toaster began the Dualit toaster range that we know today.

If design is a problem-solving activity, what are the problems that a toaster has to overcome? Before electric toasters, bread was toasted over an open fire on the end of a long fork. The bread had to hang on the end of the fork without crumbling off, and the handle of the fork had to be long enough to protect the user from having a hand too near the fire. The user controlled the toasting of the bread by eye, and the nature of the fire had a large part to play in the toasting process. A newly lit fire would generate too little heat and too much smoke, whereas the embers of a longer established fire would provide quick and evenly browned toast.

Designers of electric toasters have similar problems to solve, balancing the needs of the user with the available technology and the general behaviour of bread.

It is the bread that presents the biggest problem. Bread comes in a variety of shapes, sizes and textures: brown or white; sliced or unsliced; with or without crusts; square or round; as a roll, crumpet, muffin, bagel or teacake.

Covers awaiting assembly

Assembling toasters

Bread changes as it ages. Freshly baked bread is soft and crumbly while older bread becomes firmer as it dries out. A toaster has to cope with all these variations, without knowing which one it is dealing with.

Fresh bread makes crumbs. Over-toasted bread will eventually crumble, and carbonised crumbs can cause the elements to burn out. Dualit toasters have removable trays so that offending crumbs can be swiftly dispatched.

The next problem is how to keep the toast fresh and achieve the right degree of browning. The Dualit toaster can be pre-set to switch off after the chosen length of browning time, but, rather than using a pop-up facility, the toast remains inside the machine and retains some warmth to keep it fresh. A manual ejector-lever pushes the toast up when required.

A third problem that Dualit needed to address was how, where and when heat is generated. A toaster has to warm up, and then retain a steady output of heat. This heat has to be contained and kept away from the outside of the toaster so that the user doesn't get burned. Dualit toasters provide a 'coolwall' that prevents heat from reaching the outer wall of the toaster.

Dualit Toasters are available with a 'white heat' or 'black heat' element. The black heat element provides a long-life, energy saving option, using a heat-resistant material originally developed for the Space Shuttle. Constantly reviewing each part of the machine, Dualit have developed a new range that restrains movement within the elements, thus reducing stress and eventual burn-out. Furthermore the user can choose how many slots to switch on.

Toasters in the production line

Covers after spraying in a selection of colours

Finally there is the problem of styling. Toasters have reflected changing kitchen styles. This infers a built-in obsolescence matched by a low price. The Dualit toaster was originally made for the more industrial end of the market where styling was not such a priority. Chromed and hand-made, its reputation soon spread. Its industrial appearance attracted the atention of 'opinion formers' in the shape of magazine stylists and shop-window dressers and it soon migrated successfully into the consumer market. The design company INDES now works with Dualit, advising on styling changes and guarding the brand.

Made by hand in Southwark, London, the Dualit range is not produced by a huge company factoring parts in the Far East for cheap mass production. Every Friday each Dualit employee is provided with the necessary components to assemble a week's worth of toasters: usually twenty per operative per day. The operative's clock-card number goes on the name-plate of every toaster, so that a fault can be traced back and rectified. A repair service is also provided.

The company manufacture a wide range of products, including kettles, sandwich toasters, soup kettles, coffee makers, juicers and a corkscrew. It is for toasters, however, that they are best known. The company remains within its founder's family. The current Managing Director, Leslie Gort-Barten, speaks of the Dualit toaster as 'a shiny post-war icon of modernity that is built to operate 24 hours a day and (depending on the model) has an output of 60 to 200 slices an hour. A touch over-powered for domestic use, perhaps, but then Porsche still sell cars with a top speed of 170mph.'

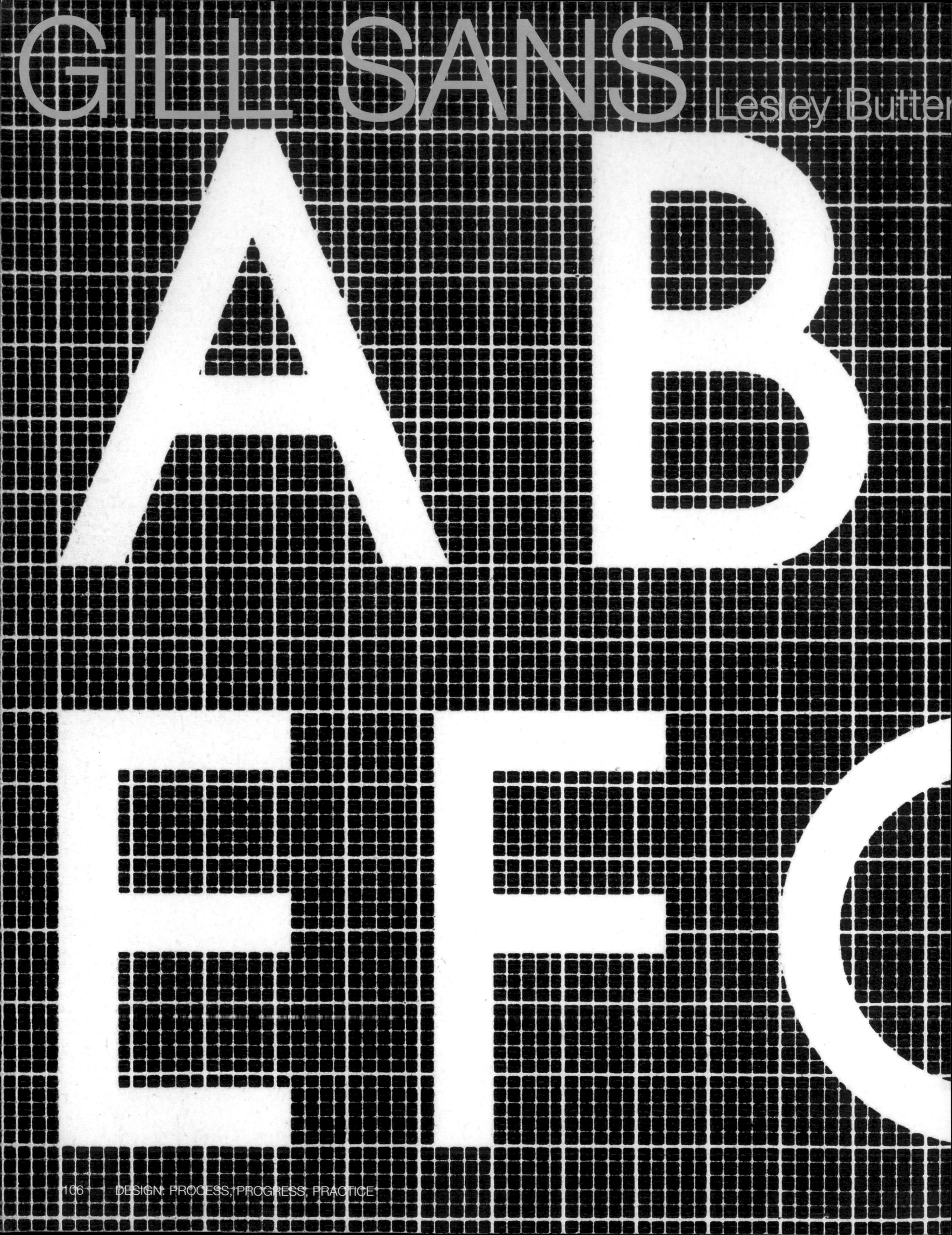

GILL SANS

Lesley Butter

th

This, previous and following pages: Gill Sans, as drawn by Eric Gill, c.1926

Typography, the style and appearance of printed material, can be linked to the development of writing. Our alphabet is believed to have originated in the eastern Mediterranean during the year 2000 BC and can be studied through illuminated books and manuscripts. Paper was invented in China, and the first paper mill established in Spain AD 1150. In 1041 the first examples of moveable type were found in China, but the Chinese language, comprising thousands of symbols, could not easily make use of moveable type. It was Johannes Gutenberg (1398-1468), a goldsmith living in Mainz, who was to develop the cutting of individual letters in metal which could be assembled into words, printed from, and then reassembled. Gutenberg was aware that if his work was to be acceptable it had to look like the work of the scribes. To achieve this he had to cut several versions of each letter to simulate the versions within the script from which he was working. By 1476, William Caxton had introduced printing to Britain, and by the beginning of the sixteenth century the trade of the scribe had been usurped by that of the printer-publisher. By the eighteenth century types were no longer copies of handwritten letters, but were shapes designed in their own right, created by chisel, for the printing technology available.

During the first half of the twentieth century typography responded to the teachings of the Bauhaus, and to Modernism. The sans serif was introduced

during the early twentieth century, when German designers were exploring the need for a typeface that they thought would represent their own time. The serif is a small stroke added to the ends of roman letters that help bind them together as words. Removing the serif provided a bolder image that was in keeping with the ethos of Modernism. By the second half of the century the introduction of commercial filmsetting and the advances of offset-lithography had transformed the profession yet again. Until this time, any history of type design would assume that letters were cut in relief and cast in metal. Now typography is a digitised message stored in a computer.

Typography is possibly the most widespread of all the arts, but needs to be the most discreet. If the type distracts from the content, then it has failed. Typography is lettering adapted for a special purpose, and is strongly influenced and informed by drawing. All typography stems from the shapes of our alphabets and numbers.

The first priority of typography must be its readability. A successful page depends upon the balanced distribution of lights and darks, and thick or thin lines. Most of the recognition of a type takes place in the top half.

Each letter has its own essential nature. There is a borderline inside which a letter, for example, a B, can have many variations, even distortions, and yet still remain integrally a B. At some point, the borderline is crossed, and a letter ceases to be itself. This issue is addressed in Eric Gill's *Essay On Typography* written in 1936.

Computers have given everyone a choice of typefaces at their fingertips. Looking not just at the choice of typefaces on a computer, but at the great variety of type we contend with in the media, the question of how many typefaces we need is often asked.

Eric Gill was born in Brighton in 1882 and attended art school in Chichester where his talent for drawing was nurtured. He became a pupil of Edward Johnston, attending his lettering classes, and accepting his life-long tenet that letters are meant to be read. By 1903 Gill had embarked upon a career as a self-employed craftsman, specialising in sculpture and the carving of lettering. Gill's views of, and position within, the discipline

of typography mirrored the tension within the profession between those who saw it as an art form, and those who saw it as a business.

In 1925 Gill started drawing alphabets for Stanley Morison of the Monotype Corporation. Monotype refers to a typesetting machine that casts and sets up type in individual characters, as opposed to Linotype which consists of a composing machine producing lines of words as single strips of metal. Gill's first typeface for Morison was called Perpetua. Gill was initially mistrustful of machine-cutting, so Morison turned his drawings into type by hand-cutting. However Gill was eventually to change his mind on this issue, and became increasingly fascinated by the mechanical processes involved. Although initially sceptical about modern typography and the use to which it was put, Gill was later to point out: 'There are now about as many different varieties of letters as there are different types of fools. I am myself responsible for designing five different sorts of sans serif letters - each one thicker and fatter than the last because every advertisement has to try and shout down its neighbours.' This perhaps explains the need for a growing repertoire of typefaces. Clients seeking corporate identity need novelty and exclusivity; Gill was increasingly aware of this fact.

Gill Sans is one of eleven type faces that Gill was to design, but it is the only one to bear his name. Stanley Morison's commission for a sans serif type was not the first. Frank Pick had commissioned Edward Johnston to design a sans serif type for exclusive use by London Underground. This initiative had inspired several further attempts to design a typeface simple enough to be drawn by anyone with a ruler and compasses,

and an ability to follow instructions. Gill was already working on a commission from the Army and Navy Stores, which needed 'absolutely legible-to-the-last-degree letters, letters which any fool can copy accurately and easily'.

Gill Sans was designed for type and machine punch cutting. Gill wanted as much mathematical measurement as possible, and little reliance on the sensibility of the craftsman. It began life as an alphabet of capitals, and was never intended for use in a novel or text book. It was intended for jobs where clear, direct information was to be conveyed. It was important for a sans serif typeface to have an even weight of line throughout, with little contrast between thick and thin, and to have as many interchangeable components as possible; for example, the bowls of the b, g, p and d etc. The problem with the creation of sans serif was that this reduction in differences risked increasing the similarities and making the overall type less legible.

Gill Sans was first cut by Monotype in 1927, and although it recieved a lukewarm reception at a trade conference in 1928, it was seen as a great success when it appeared in the public domain in 1930. By 1937 the London and North Eastern Railway had adopted Gill Sans for all its signs, timetables and publicity.

FIREWORKS: THE WARIMONO

Warimono

SHELL Lesley Butterworth

The design processes and practices within the firework industry are concerned not only with recipe and construction, but with the system of presentation, firing, and ultimate destruction. As both a designed object and system, the firework is the antithesis of sustainable design and the epitome of built-in obsolescence.

Gunpowder was probably formed and discovered by chance when charcoal, saltpetre and sulphur were mixed together and somehow ignited. Gunpowder originated in the East, either in China or India, and was recorded in England by Roger Bacon, a friar of the thirteenth century. The uses to which gunpowder could be put soon became obvious, both for firework cermonies and entertainments and for warfare.

By 1500 fireworks were being used in the East and in Europe for public events, religious festivals and in the theatre. The earliest record of a firework display in England was at Warwick Castle in 1572 to mark the visit of Queen

Elizabeth 1. Two schools of firework making and display developed in Europe: the Ruggieri brothers in Italy and France, and, in Germany, the masters of Nuremberg: Hoch, Müller and Miller.

The Ruggieri brothers created elaborate machines, or structures, such as castles, richly decorated and lit from within by collections of small fireworks which added to the creations, rather than being a display in themselves. In northern Europe effect was created by the arrangement and firing of the fireworks themselves.

Private firework companies began operating in mainland Europe, but in England fireworks and firing were in the hands of the artillery officers, until the advent of pleasure gardens in the eighteenth century when firework displays became regular items on the programme. The new and expanding business encouraged small manufacturers to get involved, and the Brock family, based in South London, were particularly successful. By the nineteenth century manufacturers were competing with each other to win contracts for displays to mark public and national victories and celebrations. As the century progressed scientific and technological developments presented fireworkers with a better understanding of chemical reaction, and different effects and a wider range of colours became available. The addition of metals such as aluminium and magnesium gave increased brilliance, and the discovery of potassium chlorate created a brighter colour palette.

Exciting and spectacular as the big displays were, and still are today, they are more useful as a means of publicity than for making a great profit. In Britain over 90% of fireworks are sold in the six week leading up to 5 November. This is mirrored by a similar trend in the USA in the period before Independence Day in July.

Fireworks are dangerous if handled incorrectly. Legislation over the years has created strict control over the packing, handling and selling of fireworks. In the UK the sale of shells to the public was banned in 1996, and 'bangers' were banned in 1997.

China, considered the birthplace of gunpowder and firework-making, leads the world in terms of the volume of production and export. The invasion of low-priced Chinese fireworks into every firework-making country has had a great effect on domestic production. Kimbolton Fireworks is one of only two remaining producers in the UK today.

To the everyday observer of a typical firework display, the differences between one country and another, or one rocket and another, are probably negligible. But the expert pyrotechnist would have an understanding of what the manufacturer was trying to achieve, the problems they would have encountered, not least to do with weather and location, and to what extent success had been achieved. A critical appraisal would be made between the quality of the colour of the stars and whether shells had burst before or after zenith had been reached.

The shell is the container of the stars, fuse and bursting charge. Separate from the shell is the firing tube, or mortar, used to get the shell into the air. The shell comes in a variety of shapes,sizes and types: round, cylindrical and repeating shells. The greatest skill of the firework maker is in the manufacture of the shells. In the case of the round shells two different methods are used to burst them: Poka, and Warimono.

Warimono, (meaning chrysanthemum in Japanese) draws a chrysanthemum-like flower in the sky by driving light stars, or smoke stars in all directions. Poka is named after the quieter sound of the considerably weaker explosion of its shell. Commonly used for deploying parachutes or tissue flags, its purpose is simply to throw out the contents into the sky. Warimono shells have a large bursting charge and a strong outer shell which aids the charge's action. The Warimono shell is constructed with four main parts, the shell, the stars, the bursting charge and the fuse.

The outer shell acts not only as the container for the stars and the bursting charge, but also helps and adjusts the ejecting force of the bursting charge.

Within the shell are two layers. The strength of the inner shell is not important, so newspaper or card is used. The outer shell is made of many layers of Japanese kozo or craft paper, which give a suitable velocity to the stars on bursting.

The structure of a shell is as follows: at the centre is the bursting charge, contained within a paper bag. The paper bag has to be very strong to prevent the bursting charge making contact with the stars during arrangement. The stars (the coloured elements of the firework) form a continual layer between the inner shell and the bursting charge. The inner shell is only a container. The outer shell is more critical, as mentioned earlier.

The fuse is inserted from outside the shell, right into the bursting charge. The fuse is fixed to the inside of the shell with hemp to prevent fire entering the shell on shooting. The outside end of the fuse is protected by a paper cap, registering the name of the shell. The fuse is ignited on its outside end by the flame on the lifting charge in the mortar on shooting. It keeps a delay time until the shell reaches a desired height in the sky and ignites the bursting charge just after the delay time has passed.

The stars are ignited by the explosion of the bursting charge, and fly like the petals of a chrysanthemum flower, burning on the surface. The burning charge is ignited by the fuse and breaks the shell into small pieces by the explosion, which ignites the stars and ejects them outwards in all directions.

This describes the process for a single-petalled chrysanthemum. Double-petalled or multi-petalled chrysanthemums are more complex. A double-petalled chrysanthemum has a second set of stars mixed in with the bursting charge. The stars placed at the centre do not fly so far, and burn out quicker. Multi-petalled chrysanthemums have alternate layers of stars and bursting charges; again, the inner stars have the shortest duration.

The bursting charge for Warimono should have a large explosive force and proper burning rate. When the burning rate is too large the shells are destroyed, or not ignited. When it is too low, there is a lack of radius of fire.

Stars can be divided into two groups; light stars for night-time use and smoke stars for daylight displays. Stars are balls of varying sizes which create the colour in the display. Each star is a ball of 'composition', the generic term for all pyrotechnic mixtures. Smoke stars are often used at night to

give a mystical effect. In general stars are formed out of a coloured fire or smoke composition, in which a quantity of binder is mixed. There are two kinds of binder: water soluble, such as glutinous rice starch, gum arabic and dextrine, and those insoluble in water, such as shellac. The stars have to be mixed and dried before they are ready to be placed in the shell.

Colour-creating materials are an essential part of fireworking. Each colour presents its own problems. Strontium carbonate creates the best red, but too high a percentage in the composition gives off too much smoke. Strontium nitrate does not produce so much smoke, but it is prone to absorbing moisture. Yellow is created by borax, or sodium oxalate which gives a clear reddish yellow. Copper sulphate gives a good blue, but not as good as Paris green. Paris green is easily scattered into the air, which is a

clockwise from right:

Preparing individual fireworks – putting chemicals into seperate tubes, then using a tube press; preparations for a firing; Warimono shell and fuse; a nest of chemical sieves; Warimono shells in storage in a modern steel store; Warimono shell and maker

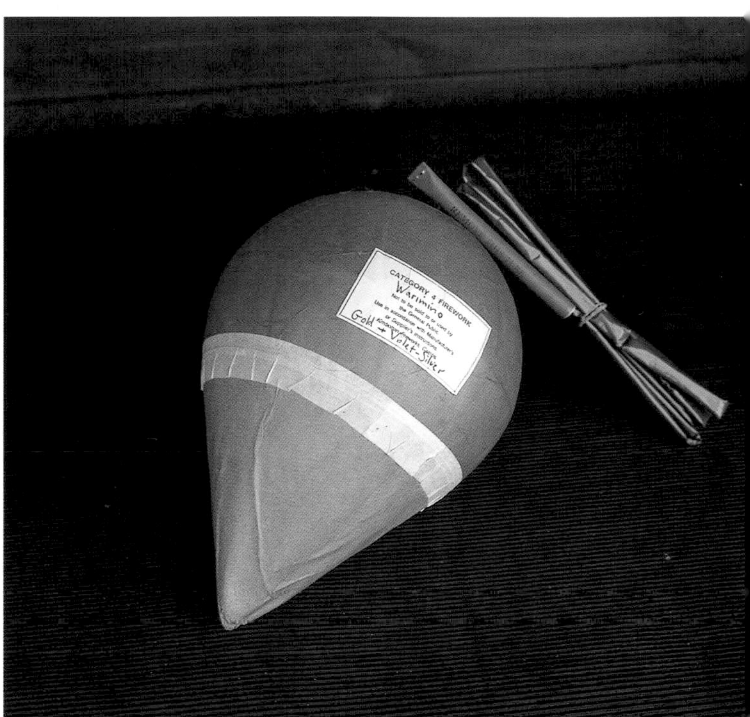

problem for fireworkers as it is poisonous. Barium chlorate gives a deep green, but creates smoke. Barium nitrate has little smoke, but not such a good colour.

In fireworking, progress used to be judged by the creation of new effects. Set piece patterns or different colour changes could be researched, developed and displayed. Today, progress is measured in terms of the spectacle that can be created, using musical and laser enhancement, and sophisticated electronic firing devices. The popularity of fireworks does not diminish, but with so few manufacturers left in any country, fewer young people are learning the skills of a successful pyrotechnist, so the future of the industry is in doubt.

THE AK47 ASS

Edward C. Ezell*

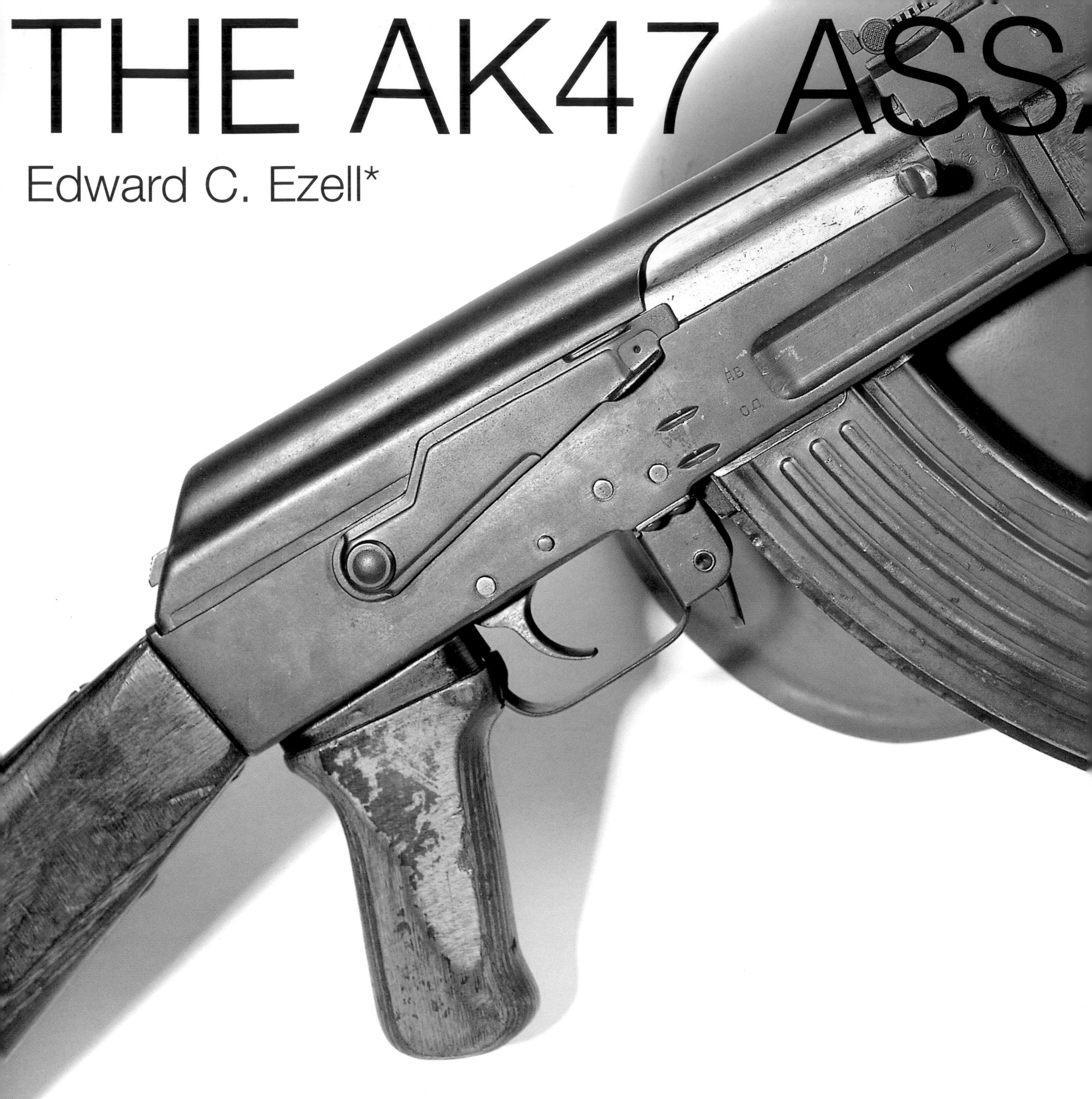

ULT RIFLE

Between thirty and fifty million AK47 rifles and its variants have been manufactured since the design was introduced in 1947. A dozen countries have manufactured versions of it. At least fifty-five nations (and an untallied number of guerrilla and terrorist organisations) use these guns daily. It is without doubt the most widely distributed and best known military shoulder weapon in the world.

The secrecy surrounding the development of weapons in any country – let alone the Soviet Union – obscures the precise details of much of the design process. Nevertheless, the development of the AK47 presents an interesting example of historical, political and technological factors influencing design and of a designer working in a creatively, if not commercially, competitive environment, resulting in a design that has lasted for over half a century.

Russia's first automatic assault rifle predated the AK47 by thirty years. The Model 1916 Federov Avtomat was designed by Vladimir Grigorevich Federov and was first used in action in the middle of the First World War. Earlier Federov had designed, with Vasily Alekseyevich Degtyarev,

M.T. Kalashnikov, aged 23

the first Russian self-loading rifle that was not simply a modification of an existing breech loader. This weapon fired a rimmed cartridge 7.62 x 54 mm (the diameter of the projectile x the length of the cartridge case), the same as fired by the standard Russian bolt action rifle. However, Federov realised that this was too powerful for an automatic rifle: the recoil forces were too high for the weapon to be properly controlled.

The cartridge Federov selected for his avtomat was the Japanese Arisaka 6.5 x 50.5 mm semi-rimmed rifle cartridge. The Russian military had experienced its effectiveness in the Russo-Japanese war of 1905 and had subsequently bought a large supply. However, although the Federov Avtomat was in use up to 1928, only 3,200 were produced.

Once the civil war began to wind down and the demand on arms factories for large-scale production of rifles began to slacken, Federov, Degtyarev and others began once again to work in earnest on assault rifle designs, and presented a number of models for trial. The specification, never fully realised, was for a 4 kg semi-automatic and automatic rifle with a magazine holding 50 rounds (soon lowered to 25) using the old 7.62 x 54 mm cartridge, which would replace the bolt action rifle, the Model 1891/30. Two designs emerged: Sergei Gavrilovich Simonov's AVS36 and Fedor Vasil'evich Tokarev's SVT38. Despite the considerably higher production costs of the SVT38, which had 25 more parts and weighed half a kilogramme more than its rival, it was declared by Stalin himself that the SVT38 would be accepted into the arsenal. However, it could not be produced fast enough to replace production of the old Model 1891/30 rifle. Shortcomings led to a modified version, the SVT40, of which over one and a third million were produced between 1940 and 1942.

However, the problems with the 7.62 x 54 mm cartridge that Federov had identified were not solved by either Simonov or Tokarev's design. This cartridge was good for fixed position warfare (as seen in much of the First World War). Indeed most standard infantry rifles of the 1939-45 era were capable of delivering a fatal shot at ranges of over 1,200 metres. The heavy charges in the cartridges needed to achieve this produced a considerable recoil and indeed they made both the AVS36 and the AVT40 unmanageable when fired as fully automatic weapons. The solution was not to be found in the smaller pistol cartridges used in sub-machine guns, which, although they made rapid fire possible, had limited striking power and so were only effective at close quarters.

The Russian military were to experience, on the receiving end, the effectiveness of automatic fire in the hands of advancing troops armed with assault rifles, such as the Haenel 7.92 x 33 mm MKb42. Clearly, a new 'intermediate' cartridge was needed that would kill effectively in an automatic weapon at a maximum range of three to four hundred metres.

The cartridge eventually judged the best technical solution had been developed by N. M. Elizarov and B. V. Semin and was adopted as the 7.62 x 39 mm Model 1943 cartridge. Yet curiously, the first weapon adopted that used this cartridge was not an automatic but a semi-automatic, designed by Simonov, the SKS45.

The new ammunition had been developed. All that was needed was the new automatic weapon to make the best use of it.

Romanian troops carrying AKMs fitted with special handgrips

By the time the new cartridge was adopted, a young technician at Ensk military small arms proving ground was beginning his career as a weapons designer. Mikhail Timofeyevich Kalashnikov had served as a tank commander at the battle for Bryansk in September 1941 when his T34 tank was hit by a German shell, a splinter of which seriously injured his shoulder. Recovering in hospital, his wardmates provided endless tales of the superiority of German weapons. He asked the hospital librarian for all the books he could find on small arms. Amongst the material lend to him was Federov's *Evolution of Small Arms*. As Kalashnikov recalled, 'The book by Vladimir Federov proved to be invaluable. It gave me my first insight into the principles of developing automatic firearms...'

During six months' convalescence leave in his home town of Alma-Ata, Kalashnikov developed a design for a sub-machine gun. He contacted a train driver he'd known from his own days as an employee on the Turkestan-Siberian Railroad who worked as a machinist in his spare time. He told his friend: 'I've already devised something. But on paper it is not all clear, so I need to build a model. That's where you come in.'

After three months the model was complete and it impressed the local party secretary enough for him to arrange for Kalashnikov to develop it at the Moscow Aviation Institute. Although ultimately the weapon was turned down, it brought him to the attention of the Chair of Infantry Weapons at Dzerzhinskiy Artillery Academy, who noted '... the great energy, and labour invested in the invention, and the originality shown in solving a series of technical problems forces us to take a close look at Comrade Kalashnikov as a talented self-educated individual to whom it is desirable to give the opportunity of a technical education. Undoubtedly he can be developed into an

excellent designer if he receives proper guidance and is put on the right path.'

As a result, he moved to the Ensk proving ground. He worked on modifications to P. M. Goryunov's machine guns and was working on sub-machine guns as late as 1948. Early in 1944 he was given some Model 1943 7.62 x 39 mm cartridges for examination, and a colleague made the suggestion that, as many other designers were working on automatic weapons for this cartridge, he should also have a go.

However, it was not Kalashnikov, but A. I. Sudayev who designed the first automatic rifle firing the new ammunition, at the beginning of 1944. Unfortunately, tests indicated that its operating parts would not withstand its heavy recoil. Even a radically redesigned second version proved too heavy. The opening was still there for another design.

Kalashnikov wrote: 'I had long been undecided about engaging in work on a new avtomat. It still seemed "experienced designers and gunsmiths are already working on this, will you be able to say a new word, to make a better system?" But the knowledge that many of my "threatening rivals" had sometimes felt the same way, let me begin on my path. And my audacity increased ... again on sheets of drawing paper more and more variants of new designs appeared.'

He identified the main challenge as developing an operating system that could be used in a variety of automatic weapons. 'The new avtomat had to be made reliable in operation, compact, light in weight, and simple in design. But what design path should I follow?'

He rejected the recoil operation employed in the blow-back type sub-machine guns. Sudayev's avtomat had incorporated this but the new cartridge required a massive bolt, adding to the weight of the weapon. Instead, Kalashnikov reported, 'I decided to establish a system of gas operated automatic weapons... Gradually, the shape of the future avtomat began to appear on the paper. Even an insignificant change in the shape of the dimensions of one part made it necessary to make changes in all of the drawings previously made. But finally a rough design of my avtomat was ready.'

The proposal package of drawings was duly sent off early in 1946 to the Main Artillery Commission in Moscow for evaluation. News soon came back that the design had been selected for development as an experimental weapon. Kalashnikov now assembled a group of designers and engineers to help prepare a more refined package of engineering drawings. 'Days passed filled with stress and hard work. We looked at each new part with excitement, carefully fitting each one to the others. Finally, after the passage of much time, we held in our hands the avtomat glistening with lacquer and grease.' It seems in fact that several test models were built and that the design continued to evolve up to 1948.

The project was immensely aided by the people and resources assigned to it. 'This first rate help speeded up my work, cutting the time in half. What had once been just lines in a drawing was now reality. But how would it behave on the firing range?'

'Testing is a very important moment in the life of a designer, and in the life of the weapon created by him ... Not everything that is good on paper is right in the testing. And so it was with our avtomat. In spite of the fact that the initial shots demonstrated the positive qualities of our new weapon, a number of design flaws appeared.' But the flaws were not serious enough to halt the testing programme and one day in 1949, Engineer-Colonel Vladimir Sergeyevich Demin burst into Kalashnikov's study in his design bureau and cried: 'Today you must dance, Mikhail Timofeyevich. The "Avtomat Kalashnikova" has been been accepted as a standard weapon'.

So after more than four years of design and engineering work, the Soviet Army adopted the 7.62 1947g, and Kalashnikov had earned the title 'Comrade Designer'.

This however was not the end of the development of the AK47. The USSR, like every other nation fighting the Second World War, suffered from a lack of raw materials, machinery and skilled workers. One step towards overcoming these obstacles was the intensive application of sheet-metal stamping production processes instead of machined assemblies worked from solid-steel stock. Kalashnikov had designed the rifle to be manufactured on sheet-metal stamping machinery. I however, for reasons not entirely clear, around 1951 a second model of the AK47 was produced with a machined-steel receiver.

Although it has been speculated that the riveted and welded joints in the original stamped metal receiver weakened after extended use, there is no evidence for this. An alternative explanation is that in the postwar rearmament, the makers of tanks and aircraft had more political clout than the small arms factories. Since the latter still had large quantities of traditional metal working machinery it was easier for them to modify the manufacturing process than to get tool and die makers for the sheet metal presses. This second model was in turn replaced by a third some time in 1953 or 1954. This included a number of improvements, such as the method of fixing the buttstock and strengthening the magazine with stamped ribs. It is this third model that is generally recognised around the world as the AK47.

This third model was produced up to 1959 when it was replaced by the Modernizirov avtomat Kalashnikova (AKM). The AKM returned to a sheet-metal receiver, reducing the weight from 4.3 to 3.14 kg. As a more accurate weapon the rear sight was recalibrated from a maximum range of eight hundred metres to one thousand.

The final version was a light machine gun version, the Ruchno Pulemet Kalashnikova (RPK), adopted in 1961 as the squad-level assault support weapon. It was essentially an AKM with a longer barrel and a larger magazine.

That these weapons were so successful was not because Kalashnikov had designed radically new elements. His genius lay in the recombining of known design elements in a reliable and durable package and the inclusion of a number of human touches. For example, the safety/fire lever can be operated by a soldier wearing heavy arctic mittens. Chromium-plating the barrels and chambers extended their life and cut down on cleaning. In creating such a rugged and easy-to-maintain rifle, Kalashnikov and his team solved the age-old problem of making a weapon that will withstand the abuse of the men and women who use it.

*Summarised by Eric Kentley from Edward Clinton Ezell's *The AK47 Story: Evolution of the Kalashnikov weapons*, Harrisburg, PA: Stackpole Books, 1986.

AK47, Pakistan border

DESIGNING AN THE CARNIVAL OF JOE FARCUS

Peter Quartermaine

Carnival Ecstasy

'Whatever you see on board, I have designed it.'

Joe Farcus, April 1999

The construction of a three-dimensional, self-supporting, and inhabitable structure – what we loosely term 'architecture' – is the most challenging form of design. It is an environment in which people must work (or sleep, or play) for long hours; any mistakes made by the architect in the process of design will be quickly felt by those who have to live in the final product. Such practical considerations are greatly increased in designing a modern cruise ship, a very large construction not usually thought of, in its entirety – discos and all – as 'architecture' (it moves), nor even as 'naval architecture' (very technical). Yet a cruise ship may accommodate a multinational 'population' of some 4000 passengers and 1500 crew. Such 'ship architecture' is self-contained, self-propelled, and must meet stringent safety standards laid down by international maritime authorities, conditions first drawn up after the sinking of the *Titanic* in April 1912.

Every stage of design takes full account of the extreme conditions a vessel may encounter at sea; ships are typically approximately one third lighter than land-based structures of comparable size (excess means higher fuel costs and lost carrying capacity), yet are extraordinarily strong and efficient. One delight of cruise ship design and building is that only the highest grade basic materials are acceptable, but the challenge for the designer is still to produce a vessel which is safe, efficient, distinctive, and enjoyable to be on. These are the logical priorities for Joe Farcus, designer of ships for the largest and most successful cruise company in the world, Carnival Cruises of Miami, USA. To date he has planned three refits, thirteen new vessels, four prototypes (designs for a new class of vessel) and advised on the design of several ships for the Holland America Line in conjunction with the Dutch architects VFD. He is 'actively working' on six cruise liners which are being built in Finland and Italy, and has been involved in discussions with Cunard on a possible new liner.

The parent organisation of Carnival Cruises, The Carnival

Joe Farcus at work

Corporation, recently acquired Cunard in Britain, giving them the prestigious liner *QE2*, as well as the largest European operator, Costa Cruises of Italy; they already owned Holland America, Seabourn and Windstar Cruises, and have a controlling interest in the UK travel company Airtours (a vital link for 'feeding' the cruise hub of Miami). On the company's twenty-first anniversary in 1995 over one million people cruised on Carnival-owned ships, while their crews are drawn from over thirty countries. The Carnival fleet of self-styled 'fun ships', of which the 1996 *Carnival Destiny* and her sisters are the largest, is among the world's most modern, and every one of its fourteen vessels, as well as those now under construction, is the creation of Joe Farcus. The company began very modestly in Miami with one second-hand ship, but today it keeps Farcus fully occupied designing every aspect of new ships for its growing fleet. His best-known single artefact, though, must be the company's distinctive winged funnel, which first appeared on the new liner *Tropicale* in 1981.

Farcus is 54, and graduated in architecture from the University of Florida at Gainesville in 1967. He then worked for a time with the well-known Miami architect Morris Lapidus, designer of hotels, before the office was invited in the early 1970s to submit proposals for the refit of Carnival's second vessel, the former transatlantic liner *Empress of Britain* (1960), which was to become their *Carnivale*. At this time Farcus met Ted Arison, founder of the company, and subsequently did some work in his apartment. When in 1977 Carnival acquired their third ship, the *Festivale* (originally the 1961 *Transvaal Castle*, later Safmarine's *SA Vaal*), Farcus proposed to Arison that he should do the design work for that refit. After an initial all-day meeting, Farcus volunteered to submit some ideas for the next day, and, as he still recalls, worked through the night to produce detailed proposals for a restaurant and the main theatre. Acceptance of his ideas took him to Europe within two weeks (only his second visit) and later to Japan for the two

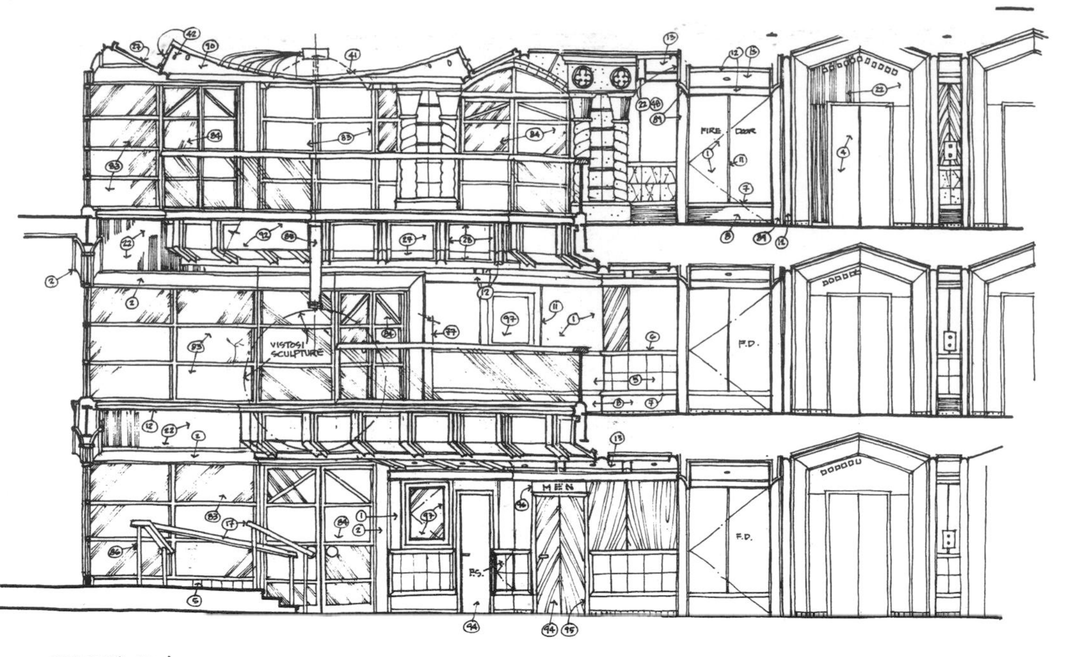

Hand-drawn section by Joe Farcus.

month refit. He has never looked back: 'Carnival have kept me busy.'

Farcus is arguably the most prolific designer in the history of the profession, and his practical skills, together with an affectionate understanding of ships and a sure hand at drawing, make him perhaps the most original. Each day he works long hours in the small upstairs studio across the courtyard of his Miami Beach home, drawing by hand from imagination – but in detail and to scale on squared paper – every elevator, staircase, light fitting and sushi bar of vast, and vastly complex, cruise ships for transmission by fax to shipbuilders and subcontractors in Finland and Italy. These periods of intense productivity in the studio (punctuated constantly by faxes, telephone calls, computer link transmission of ship plans, and video exchange of accommodation mock-ups and samples of materials) alternate with visits every five or six weeks to shipyards, factories and workshops in Europe.

Each vessel will cost almost US$500 million to construct at 1999 prices, so this is popular product design on a grand scale, but in his method of working Farcus has 'pretty much settled down into the old-fashioned way, working freehand in pen and ink'. It sounds easy, and he makes it seem so, but as he observes – while demonstrating a new Computer Aided Drawing (CAD) package onscreen – 'many architects can't do that, believe it or not, because many architects simply can't draw'. It is a key point. For Farcus an ease and love of drawing, of lucidly executing detailed renderings of an envisaged three-dimensional world, lies at the very heart of his work. In his studio hangs an expressive ink drawing of the American eagle, done when he was only thirteen, and this precocious talent he now employs in designing every aspect of cruise ships – seeking to capture in his drawings something of the 'experience', as he terms it, that he hopes passengers will have – even down to choosing and designing the material and pattern of the carpets.

Atrium of the *Carnival Elation*

‘I design ships that I would love to take a cruise on,’ he explains, ‘there is no question of saying: “Well, I don’t really like this, but I think it’s right for this space”.’ In realising these environments, he finds it both quicker and more expressive – more helpful, that is, to the builders and subcontractors – to draw complex designs by hand rather than use CAD programmes. This also enables him to include in his

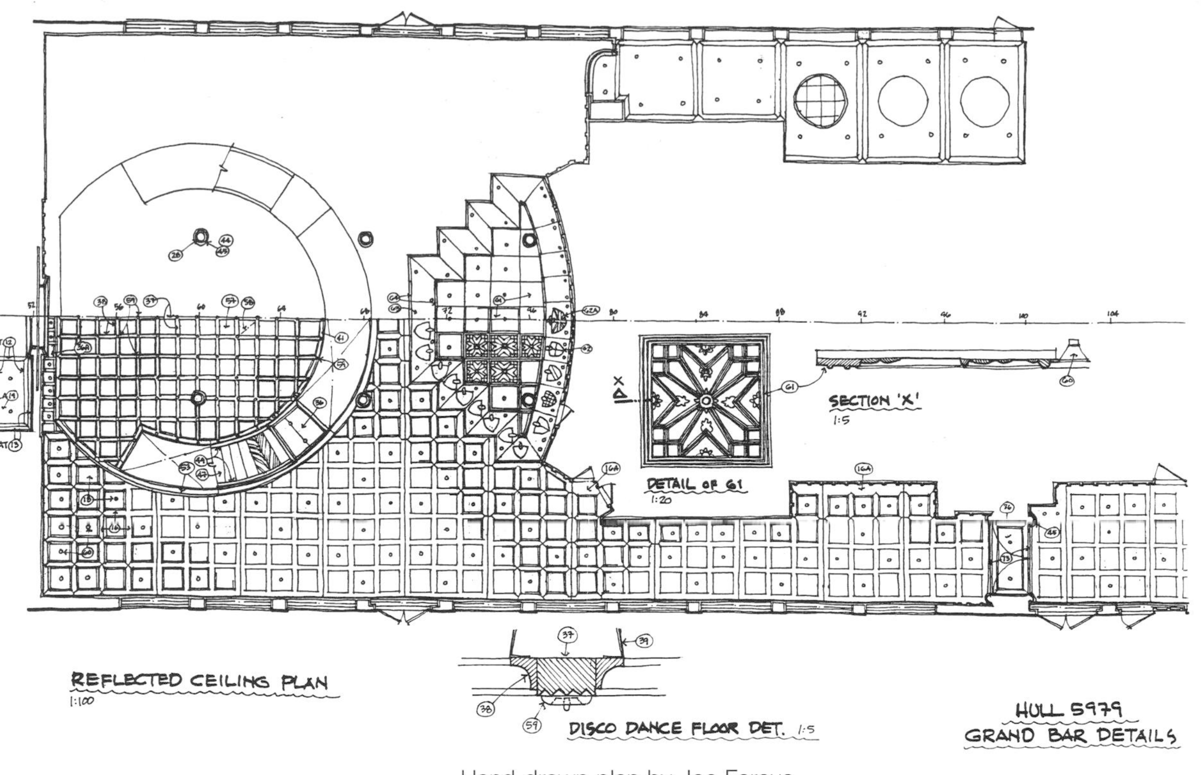

Hand-drawn plan by Joe Farcus.

graphic work, which importantly he regards as ‘finished drawings, not just architectural plans’, precise but economical indications of materials and texture which enable the shipbuilders and their subcontractors immediately to gain an impression of what these spaces should look like. He tries to ‘imbue these drawings not only with the architectural necessities, but also the feeling of the room’. Carnival Cruises Technical Services provide expert backup at every stage, but because Farcus himself also understands the functional relationship between his designed visible environments and the steel fabric of the ship proper, the numbered annotations to his drawings both help the subcontractors – ‘the people who use their own skills to find clever ways of constructing what I have designed’ – and enable him to answer their queries directly, without the need (as with larger design teams) for several people to consult before agreeing a solution. Equally, though, cooperation is for him the way to achieve the best result possible – ‘you give a little, but you get’ – and this demands the ability to work closely with builders at several levels in different countries.

Farcus works with a strong sense of maritime tradition and is also involved in initial decisions affecting the overall disposition of space within the hull; it is an ideal combination for evolutionary yet practical design (for example, the adoption of swivelling Azipod propulsion units on recent vessels has eliminated the traditional propulsion layout, with space-consuming drive shafts). Having worked with the company through the difficult early years, his unique

Carnival Destiny:
The Rotunda

relationship with Carnival gives him an unparalleled understanding of their operations. He has also been involved in planning public rooms on Holland America's *Statendam*-class liners, and the pattern of the distinctive Costa prototype at present being built in Finland will also be used for new Carnival vessels; such economies of scale give Carnival a significant advantage over competitors.

Ships have always fascinated Farcus. As a child he owned a copy of the little book by Leonard W. Sharpe entitled *How To Draw Ships* (1945, reprinted 1956), and he still treasures his well-thumbed copy. He recalls referring to Sharpe's book, among others,

during that long night of drawing up his first ship conversion proposals for Carnival, and since then, as he modestly puts it, 'I have made my hobby my career'. For Farcus, the role of the ultra-modern cruise vessel today is only fully explicable in the wider context of what he terms 'the romance of the sea'. In booking a cruise people are buying into an aspect, however vaguely defined, of our enduring fascination with ships and the sea (to the industry's surprise – and relief – bookings soared in the wake of James Cameron's film *Titanic*), and a sharp awareness of this informs how Farcus approaches cruise ship design: 'after all, the main thing with a ship is the sea'.

Every element in the design of a cruise ship is determined by planned returns on investment, but that does not mean that there is no place for opulence. Works have been commissioned from the Venetian glass sculptor Luciano Vistosi, an Egyptologist from a university in Gdansk checked the decorative hieroglyphics for the Egyptian Room on the *1989 Fantasy*, and the Sports Bar on the *Carnival Triumph*, launched June 1999 in Italy, features original medals, tickets, diplomas and posters from Olympic Games since before the turn of the century.

Farcus's aim with each vessel is to design an 'ideal city' that goes to sea, a floating environment which offers the variety, ambience and surprises of a 'real' city, but without its drawbacks. In this sense it is the ship, as much as (perhaps more than) any port, that is the destination of passengers who embark. Land-based architecture offers no parallel to the divergent yet complementary facilities of a modern cruise ship, whose designer must understand the differing requirements and potential of all interrelated facilities if the vessel is to be profitable.

Metropolis Bar

Each day Farcus liaises from Miami with shipyards and subcontractors on issues involving millions of dollars, takes decisions with them on proposed new construction and production techniques, and suggests practical compromises in the never-ending tussle between the design he has envisaged and what can practically be achieved within time and cost constraints; no ship has yet been launched exactly as he had planned it. The distinguished Swedish designer of passenger ships Robert Tillberg, whose experience goes back to the famous *Kungsholm* of 1964 but who was also the designer of P&O's new *Oriana*, once described his work as 'the greatest compromise of all'.

Behind all the other pressures is the fact that a cruise ship must turn a profit: every aspect of its design is therefore inherently linked to practicality and profitability. The giant winged funnel that Farcus created for Carnival (on the *Destiny* class a giant fibreglass moulding) not only efficiently disperses exhaust gases – something naval architects refused to believe until wind-tunnel tests were done – but proclaims the company's distinctive identity just as strongly as did the great multiple funnels (one of them often a dummy, as on the *Titanic*) of earlier transatlantic liners. Like theirs, the funnel is as much symbolic (of Miami-style modernity, colourfulness and fun) as it is strictly practical; this, too, is part of good design.

A typical designer's studio

Ships have always been the largest, and among the most complex, mobile creations of human industry; our enduring fascination with the prestigious Titanic's sinking (by no means the world's worst maritime disaster) reflects this. The role of cargo vessels in moving over 90% of international trade also remains paramount (if largely ignored) for, as John Szarkowski reminds us in *A Maritime Album* (1997), 'the best way to move something heavy from here to there was and is to float it there. This is as true now as it was in the days of Homer.' However, with the advent of containerisation in the 1960s, and the subsequent relocation of many port operations to 'greenfield' or 'bluecoast' sites, shipping movement ceased to be part of the civic and popular imagination, as it inevitably was when the River Thames beside the Design Museum (itself once a river warehouse) was an active part of the great Port of London. The American photographer and critic Allan Sekula argues persuasively in *Fish Story* (1995) that 'the metropolitan gaze no longer falls on the waterfront' and that from this industrial and cultural shift of perspective a 'cognitive blankness follows'. He believes the sea to be 'less comprehensible to today's elites than it was before 1945, in the nineteenth century, or even during the Enlightenment'. Intriguingly, it is in this context that cruising continues its extraordinary progress, with all companies heavily committed to new vessels (and still with over 90% of current holiday-makers yet to take a cruise).

Since the appearance of the first Boeing 'jetliners' on transatlantic routes in the 1960s, it has been faster and cheaper to travel by air than to take a ship. Passenger ships have vanished as transport, but now flourish for leisure cruising, offering on board almost infinitely varied leisure and entertainment environments. The phenomenal rise of Carnival reflects this change. Farcus sees himself as designing 'Entertainment Architecture' for these floating cities, creations which themselves invite comparison with those popular buildings of Las Vegas which Alan Hess characterised in *Viva Las Vegas* (1993) as 'After Hours Architecture'. Farcus, though, sees any comparison as being between a cruise ship and Vegas as a whole; he and Carnival were once approached by a hotel developer who wanted to build a 'cruise ship' to be located in Vegas, which, he feels, 'says it all'.

But real ships that carry passengers – or 'guests', as Carnival terms them – are always, in design terms, two worlds in one: alongside visible public and private spaces: restaurants, lounges, theatres, cabins, lie the skilfully hidden service and mechanical spaces - stores, kitchens, service areas, laundries, air-conditioning ducts, fresh water plants, engines, generators, sewage treatment equipment, that make possible the carefree cruises for which, as Farcus is well aware, people trade their most precious assets: time and money.

Carnival Inspiration Brasserie Bar

The public spaces that Farcus plans and furnishes demand an awareness of those invisible spaces central to the proper functioning of a ship. Meanwhile, the passenger experience afloat has always relied on the creation of a fantasy world more closely related (at least in First Class) to that of land-based architecture – marble swimming pools, armchairs and imposing fireplaces, with overhead crystal chandeliers and panelled ceilings – than to any 'nautical' tradition. Farcus's designs are not specifically themed. He says he aims for something more akin to what gives a city 'a certain individual expression which can be readily experienced and felt by the visitor'. His floating cities are 'not as serious in the scope of things, but they are extremely important to those who sail on them'. He turns to the cinema for an analogy, explaining that 'one of the pleasures of cruising is that you are part of the movie, not part of the audience'.

SOUTHWARK B DESIGN SERVIC AND THE NORT PECKHAM ESTA

Pauline Nee

Samuel Street, formerly Havant Way. Twelve new homes built to high standards of accessability and sustainability

BEFORE 'an alien and opressive environment'

AFTER selective demolition allowed construction of new secure entranceways to upper maisonettes.

Tenant consultation: an essential component of quality design

The North Peckham Estate, built in the optimistic 1960s, had, by the 1980s, developed into an alien and oppressive environment distinguished by its high crime levels. The resultant tenant fear was exacerbated by dissatisfaction with a range of design and management issues including refuse collection, car parking and dwelling layout.

Despite this widespread dissatisfaction tenants rejected government initiatives that encouraged them to sever the links with the local authority. The formation of a Housing Action Trust, which would have brought with it a funding 'dowry' to address the design and technical problems on the estate, was turned down by tenant ballot. Housing Action Trusts proved to be unpopular nationally, and were rejected in a series of ballots up and down the country. By the 1990s the Government had begun to address the extensive design, technical and social problems encountered on 1960s inner city estates through the Estate Action Programme.

Estate Action funding acknowledged the need for a comprehensive approach, based on a partnership between Central Government, tenants from the estate, the council and local business and voluntary agencies. It also established that the programme should enable the local community to take more control over its environment. Southwark Council, and North Peckham tenants, 'signed up' to that approach and in March 1992 Southwark received approval

BEFORE 'the public courtyards were dark and dank, the play areas abandoned'

AFTER demolition of east-west block allows recreation of traditional street pattern. Remodelling of maisonettes provides front doors at street level.

for the first phase of its Estate Action bid. In August 1993 it submitted proposals for a second tranche of funding, for the project known as North Peckham III. This article concentrates on the tenant consultation aspects of the North Peckham III project.

The design team appointed to work on the project was well aware that the success of the scheme depended on extensive and meaningful tenant consultation. This article and the Design Museum exhibition concentrate largely on that aspect of the process. It is worth noting that the project covered 422 homes. The contract cost was £14m and the works were scheduled to take 4 years. Obviously meaningful tenant consultation on a project of such dimensions has to be well planned and meticulously carried out.

The design of the North Peckham estate, visionary for its time, provided a totally unsuitable environment only 20 years later. Access to every home was via a second floor pedestrian deck 'pedway'. The original concept envisaged streets in the sky, protected from traffic and allowing the development of neighbourly friendships in a safe environment. The reality was a desolate pedway network ideal for opportunistic criminals. The repetition of similar blocks, decks and courtyards (taken as a whole the estate provided 1,429 homes) and the lack of visible landmarks presented visitors with an impenetrable maze. Worse, emergency services were faced with the real problem of how to find the homes of callers in need.

The original designers envisaged a car-free environment, with parking limited to multi-storey car parking blocks. While security fears meant that these blocks were largely unused their impact was oppressive and alienating. Car owners parked on service roads with the result that refuse and fire vehicles were frequently excluded while children's play areas became dangerous. The separation of vehicular and pedestrian traffic lead to increased burglary and vandalism at the largely deserted ground level.

No tenant had a front door opening onto the street and no tenant had a private garden. Parents were afraid to let their children use the play areas.

BEFORE 'a desolate pedway network, ideal for opportunist criminals'

AFTER landscaped, secure entranceway replaces access via pedway network

Walking around the North Peckham estate at ground level was a dispiriting and frequently frightening experience. The public courtyards were dark and dank, the play areas abandoned. Perversely, the success of the tree planting excluded sunshine throughout the summer, contributing to the desolation.

The overall approach to the resolution of these problems, developed in consultation with tenants, was to recreate a traditional street pattern with front doors and gardens at ground level. This was achieved by demolishing blocks with an east-west orientation and remodelling the north-south blocks to create maisonettes with doors at ground floor level. The extensive pedway network was to be eliminated, with tenants living in the upper floors sharing new entranceways, lifts and self-contained pedways with a maximum of ten other residents. Enclosed communal gardens and play areas were to be designed for tenants on the upper levels.

The Design Museum exhibition concentrates on design issues addressed and resolved with tenants. There were three particular design solutions, initiated by the tenants themselves, which contributed to the overall success of the scheme.

The overall design concept required that the pedways be sub-divided into small, self-contained areas, each with access for a maximum of twelve tenants. The design team initially proposed that the sub-division be created simply, with a wall or a railing. Tenants, however, suggested that the dividing wall could form the spine of two additional rooms so that tenants adjacent to that part of the pedway could each have an extra bedroom. The designers developed this proposal, using the front elevation of these new pedway rooms, together with the new entranceways, to modulate the otherwise monotonous elevations to the five-storey, linear blocks.

Tenants suggested that lifts were necessary to get up to the second floor maisonettes but the cost of providing lifts for groups of twelve or less tenants was prohibitive. The designers, aware of the benefits to parents with pushchairs, people with disabilities and tenants with shopping, consulted a lift manufacturer and developed the concept of a

BEFORE Havant Way (right) 'no tenant had a private garden'

AFTER 12 new homes, each with their own patio and garden

two-compartment lift, accessible from opposite sides for adjacent entranceways. The small numbers using the lift meant that sharing it was a viable solution, reducing cost while improving access for all.

The third tenant suggestion was more fundamental. The solution to the existing problems involved demolition of east-west blocks, and the remodelling of north-south blocks, to recreate a traditional street pattern. One of the blocks, Havant Way, was located to the north of the main project area, alongside lower-rise blocks. When the council decided to build three-storey housing on its other flank tenants suggested that Havant Way might 'stick out like a sore thumb' between low-rise housing on either side. Although the construction contract was already into its second year on site, tenants suggested that the block be demolished and replaced with low-rise housing. The design team costed outline sketches that the Housing Department submitted to the Government for approval. All parties saw the advantages of the tenants' proposal. The result was the design and construction of Samuel Street: twelve high-quality new homes built to extremely high standards of sustainability and accessibility.

The examples cited above illustrate that the consultation process addressed issues fundamental to the design of the scheme overall. The next section of this article outlines the processes that provided the means for this strategic input to evolve, while enabling smaller goups of tenants to influence the design of their local entrance, stairway or communal garden and individual tenants to have an input into the detailed design of their own home.

At the inception of the scheme the client and the design team met with tenants representing the whole of the North Peckham estate. At these meetings they thrashed out the general approach, taking into account lessons learnt on Phase II as well as changes in the Government's funding regime. It was essential that tenants representing all of the estate were involved at this stage, as proposals for Phase III, such as modifications to the district heating system or demolition of the car parking blocks, would have an impact

Dark, dank courtyards and deserted play areas replaced by private gardens backing onto a communal garden for upper-floor residents

'The design of the North Peckham Estate, visionary for its time, provides a totally unsuitable environment only 20 years later… the repetition of similar blocks and the lack of visible landmarks presented visitors with an impenetrable maze.'

local children 'redesign' the estate

'the design team was well aware that the success of the scheme depended on *extensive and meaningful consultation*'

on the rest of the estate. Once the general principles were established the design team began to meet with the Phase III project group. Whilst membership of this group, which met at least once a month, was open to all, a core group of tenants attended regularly, developing their understanding of the opportunities offered by the scheme. The design challenges and potential solutions were outlined using a variety of techniques including simple models, photographs, sketches and coloured diagrams. Debate at these sessions was lively and discussion meaningful. Even if they had wanted to the design team was not going to get away with glib explanations or superficial solutions.

Obviously only a small proportion of the 422 tenants attended these detailed discussions. To ensure widespread comprehension of the extent of the scheme the client arranged exhibitions, newsletters and leaflets to explain the proposals in detail. The design team then set up a series of local consultation sessions which included meetings with tenants from individual blocks to discuss issues such as the new entranceway or play provision in the communal garden; meetings with tenants from individual pedways to discuss floor and wall finishes; and finally meetings with individual tenants to discuss kitchen layout and colour schemes. These discussions where helped by the completion of two show dwellings which tenants could visit before making decisions on their own home.

Work on North Peckham III is now complete and has proved to be a great success. All parties involved are convinced that this success can, in large part, be attributed to the extensive involvement of the tenants from inception of the scheme. What the exhibition also shows, I hope, is that consultation has to be meaningful. The design team and the housing staff involved in this project encouraged consultation, took the tenants' suggestions seriously, argued against them when they felt they would not work but ran with them when they felt they would.

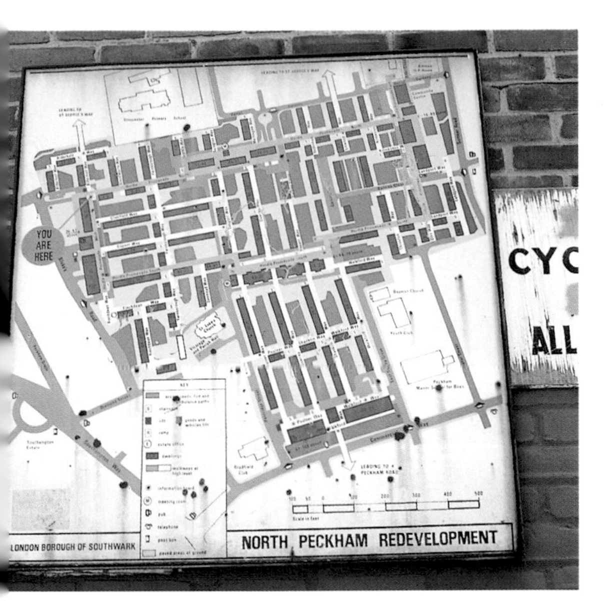

The North Peckham Redevelopment built in the optimistic 1960s

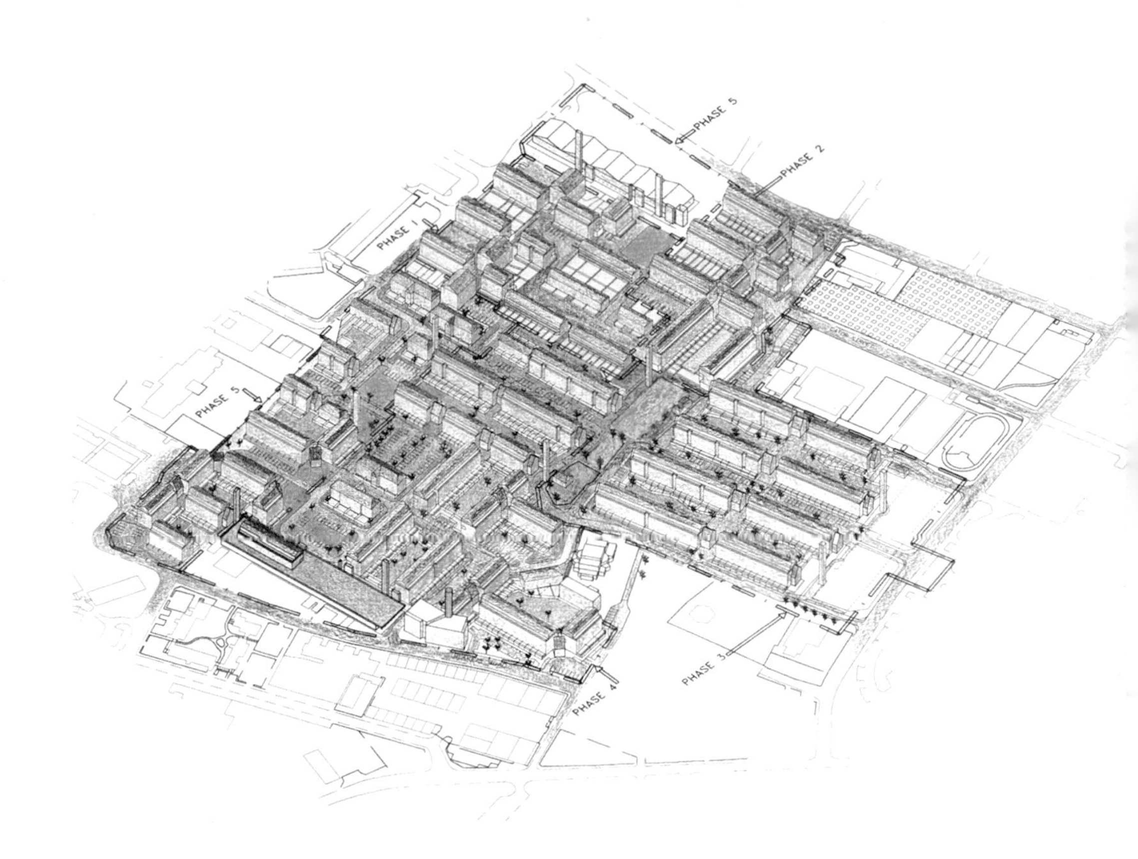

'a two-compartment lift, accessable from opposite sides for adjacent entranceways'

Photography Credits

Jefferson Smith
pp.20,104,105,116,117

Bridgeman Art Library
pp.35, 36, 37 (x2), 84 (btm.)

Branson Coates
pp.38, 40

Bonhams, London
pp.48, 51

Durrell Bishop at Itch, London
p.52

British Museum
p.78

Science and Society Picture Library, London
p.82

Alastair Hunter/British Architectural Library, RIBA, London
p.87

St. Bride Printing Library, London
p.106-111

St. Petersburg Museum of Artillery, Engineers and Signals
p.120

The Defence Picture Library, Plymouth
p.118, 122

Wayne Perry/The Defence Picture Library, Plymouth
p.125

Peter Mackertich
pp.136, 138(r.), 139(r.), 140(r.), 141(r.), 142, 145(l.)+(btm. r.)

Project credits

IDEO projects (pp.88 - 99)

1. Connected listening
Working with Audible, IDEO contributors were:
Industrial Design
Thomas Overthun
Mechanical Engineering
Sam Hu, Greg Hayes
Electrical Engineering
Scott Brenneman, Tony Rosetti
Manufacturing Liaison
Tim Billings

2. Connected learning
Working with Netschools,
IDEO contributors were:
Industrial Design
Gretchen Barnes
Engineering
Alex Kazaks and Rickson Sun

3. Digital Radio
Working with the BBC,
IDEO designers were:
Tracy Currer, Nick Dormon

4. Digital moment
Working with the Eastman Kodak Design, Usability & Engineering staff,
IDEO contributors were:
Project Lead
Larry Shubert
Interaction Design
Mat Hunter
Human Factors
Jane Fulton Suri
Industrial Design
Nick Oakley

5. Interactive keyboard
Working with Yamaha,
IDEO contributors were:
Industrial Design
Takeshi Ishiguro
Interaction Design
Hector Moll-Carillo

6. Interactive space
Working with Steelcase,
IDEO contributors were:
Project Lead
Jim Yurchenco
Industrial Design
Bob Arko
Interaction Design
Marion Buchenau
Mechanical Engineering
Chuck Seiber
Electrical Engineering
Ed Kirk

7. Expressive tastes
Designers
Frank Friedman, Naoto Fukasawa, Philip Grebe, Sam Hecht, Takeshi Ishiguro, Nick Oakley, David Peschel, Matthew Rohrbach, Gary Schultz, Christopher Weeldreyer

8. Expressive lamp
Design - Takeshi Ishiguro
(while studying at the Royal College of Art)

Southwark Building Design Service (pp.136 - 145)

North Peckham Phase III project team:
Pauline Nee (Borough Architect and Building Surveyor) Judith Jeffrey, Eoin Downing, Mike Jeffery, Barry Hurrell, Rupert King, Ted Butters, Bob Wilkin

Quantity Surveyors:
James Nisbet and Partners:
Michael Noble,
Stephen Fisher

Structural Engineers:
Sir Frederick Snow and Partners Ltd:
John Aldridge

Mechanical and Electrical:
Butler and Young Associates:
Graeme Scott
Kieron Smith
Chris Westbury

Client: Southwark Council:
Rosemary Gardens Neighbourhood Housing Office:
Steve Barnes